THE FLOATING FROG

By

Steve Rowley

Copyright © 2026

All rights reserved.

Published by:

Dedication

*Dedicated to the committee of voices in my head
who assured me this book was a good idea.*

Introduction

Just to give you an insight into the mentality of the author - before you invest time following the adventures of a somewhat very average member of the human race.

My final English Language exam did not go according to plan.

Picture the scene: an exam hall, silent as the grave. Rows of students hunched over papers, brows furrowed, pens poised. I was deep into a passage about a forest fire and its devastating effects (or is it affects?) on the local wildlife.

Then came the question responsible for this book's title, and the main reason I flunked English Language:

Question: *In your own words, explain why the author wrote: "In the morning after the fire, everything seemed peaceful. No birds were singing, just a frog was slowly floating along the stream."*

In my head, I thought: *It's quiet because all the creatures, including the birds, had been incinerated by the fire.*

But what about the floating frog?

Maybe he'd been boiled alive. Or poisoned by eating a charcoaled grasshopper.

In my panic, I opted for the agonising loneliness of losing his home and family - then ending his life by throwing himself into the water.

Logic had clearly left the building. A frog drowning? Really?

The exam ended. Still overthinking the frog's tragic demise, I turned to my mate Pete:

Me: "What was your explanation for the floating frog?"

Pete *(confused)*: "What floating frog?"

Me: "You know - the frog floating along the stream after the fire."

Pete *(shaking his head)*: "Are you serious? It said the 'fog' slowly floating along the stream."

Needless to say, I failed miserably.

I left school with no decent qualifications. My immediate career options were either cigar factory cleaner or politician, neither needed academic credentials.

I chose what I considered the honest job: Cigar Factory Cleaner.

So, without further ado, ladies and gentlemen, boys and girls, lovers of amphibians and accidental metaphors…

I present to you:

THE FLOATING FROG

Readers' Instructions

This isn't a life story - just stories from my life.

Read it front to back, back to front, inside out, outside in… Or, if you're a certified Nosey Parker, upside down.

The Tale-Truthing (where I come clean) is the epilogue - best saved for last. (Unless you're the sort who reads dessert menus first.)

Interludes & Outerludes

Interlude: Mildly interesting bits loosely connected to the tale. Perfect moment to make a cuppa before diving back in.

Outerlude: Dunk your biscuit - it's back on.

Here's a totally random example:

Interlude:

Whatever happened to the cinema ice cream ladies - the usherettes?

As a kid, I lived for that moment: five minutes before the interlude, when they'd magically materialise at the bottom of the aisle steps.

Then, waiting for the tiny light above their tray to illuminate - open for business - was more gripping than the matinée itself.

I've missed ten-minute chunks of so many films:

Five minutes watching her unveil and organise her collection of frozen jewels before the tray light moment.

Then a further five minutes once the film had resumed, as Mum attempted to scrub my latest ice cream-inspired T-shirt into something socially acceptable.

Outerlude:

Where was I…

All the characters in this book are real.

Some names have been changed - not for dramatization purposes, but purely for self-preservation.

Table of Contents

The Slide

The Real Life or Just Fantasy?

Back in the Day

Kids walked to school alone at age seven. Totally ordinary.

So, just like any other school day, my friend Ivor and I stopped at Basset Park for a couple of trips down the tall slide.

And when I say tall, I mean tall, not one of those child-friendly slides you get today. I mean a proper slide. A launchpad for chaos.

Interlude:

The park sits behind a pub that later became famous as the venue for the final scene of the UK TV comedy series *Gavin and Stacey*. But back in the sixties, the entire park was covered in black grass, what the Irish call tarmac.

To give it some texture, it had a sprinkling of loose gravel, mixed with broken glass.

And to enhance the excitement even further, it featured a twelve-inch-diameter storm drain sticking up in the middle of the park.

The perimeter was enclosed by an eight-foot-high metal railing fence, fortifying the park's security to British prison yard standards.

I was never certain whether this was to keep kids in or out.

Thinking about it, being next to a pub, it was probably designed as a kids' pen, allowing dads to safely confine their children while they went for a cheeky pint or two.

Then, after a few hours solving all the world's problems in the Pub Parliament, drinking pints of wisdom, it would be time to adjourn. The dads would leave the pub, head to the park, and release the detainees before heading home to Mum.

As long as they arrived home with the correct child of the correct sex, Dad would be praised for entertaining the kids all afternoon.

Outerlude:

Where Was I?…

Back to the slide.

Being an extremely competitive child, I was determined to be the fastest down, trying every trick imaginable to keep Ivor in second place.

Nominating myself to go first in a best-of-three competition, I climbed to the top of the slide.

I sat down, reached forward, grabbed the front of the safety bars, designed, apparently, to stop you falling off sideways.

Me: "Here we go! Two, three, four!"

Then, thrusting my body forward and yanking the bars, I launched myself down the chute, hitting Warp 1.

Strutting around the bottom of the slide, convinced I was unbeatable, I challenged Ivor to do better. The cheeky bastard hit Warp 2.

As I stood there in disbelief, I felt the back of my trousers, soggy!

I'd unknowingly wiped the damp slide with my backside and gifted Ivor a dry, record-breaking run.

OK! Time to improvise for round two.

Knowing my damp trousers would sabotage any chance of victory, I briefly considered removing them to reduce friction, but decided that walking around a kiddie's park half-naked wasn't wise.

After a quick debrief, basically pulling my wet Y-fronts from my bum, I plucked an idea out of nowhere:

Why not take off my woolly jumper, tie it around my waist, and sit on it to reduce friction to a minimum?

To implement my clever plan, I needed Ivor to go first so he couldn't copy my newly patented advancement in Slide-ology.

Even now, I'm convinced I could pitch it on *Dragon's Den*. Back to round two.

I played my ace card: last man, last man, forcing Ivor to go first. I couldn't believe it. The even bigger bastard hit Warp 3.

The pressure was on.

As I climbed the steps, my genius evolved further.

Why not tie my woolly jumper around my chest and go down headfirst, totally eliminating the slider's curse: friction.

With my jumper tied tightly around my chest, I swallow-dived onto the chute from the top step.

Physics Lesson: For the Doubters

To all the physics experts doubting my zero-friction theory, let me explain:

I completely eliminated 'slide friction' during my record attempt from top to bottom.

Here's the theory:

If you throw yourself headfirst down a slide with a woollen garment wrapped around your chest, and that garment catches on one of the guardrail bolts, the downward momentum causes the body attached to the garment to act like a pendulum, thus propelling the foolish sod off the side of the slide and onto the ground without ever touching the chute.

Hence, Zero Friction.

I can't really remember much of that journey down the slide, understandable, given I achieved a speed of Warp 4.

Yep, Warp 4. Which, even today, remains a slider's world record.

My zero-gravity journey ended abruptly when the back of my head slammed onto the Irish black grass beneath the slide.

The sudden impact sent my body into shock, masking any immediate pain.

I had transformed into Major Tom and lost contact with Ground Control.

As I lay on the tarmac, staring up at the top of the slide, I began drifting from reality.

I was mesmerised by my woolly jumper, still caught on the bolt, flapping like a flag in the wind. The sensation of warm blood trickling down my back sent me further into orbit.

Suddenly, my silent journey was interrupted by the sound of Ground Control trying to re-establish contact.

Stranger Danger: The Chase

The voice grew louder. Fantasy collapsed into reality.

Realising what had happened, I nervously ran a quick systems check: Right leg. Left leg. Right arm. Left arm.

So far, so good.

To my horror, Ground Control had turned into a man running rapidly towards me shouting:

Man: "Hey, boy! Stay there, I'm coming!"

Hearing "Hey, boy" and "I'm coming" immediately triggered 'Stranger Danger Mode'.

I jumped to my feet, bounced off the slide a couple of times, and desperately tried to coordinate my limbs.

Instinctively, I bolted in the opposite direction, away from the stranger who was still shouting:

Stranger: "Please, please stop! Let me help you!" This act of concern didn't fool me.

I might've been seven years old and slightly concussed, but I knew his intention: To chase down and help himself to his injured prey.

I ran for my life, the stranger in hot pursuit.

I zigzagged around the park, dodging capture like a pint-sized Jason Bourne. Soon, we reached the storm drain.

After a frantic few laps around it, playing 'Dodge the Pedo', he finally gave up the chase and stopped.

There we were: face to face, with only the storm drain between us. Frightened and shaking, I stared at him in horror.

He returned a similar look, but with added beads of sweat and a very pale face.

Sweaty Stranger *(pleading)*: "Please, son, let me help you. I was in my car and saw what happened. Please let me take you home."

Thanks to public information films like *Charley Says*, I knew:

"Always tell your mummy before talking to strangers."

I instinctively filed him under puppy breeder, not Good Samaritan.

In my mind, I was determined not to give him the chance to show me any cute puppies.

After what felt like the longest staring contest in history, I made a break for the park exit, shouting:

Me *(cry shouting)*: "Leave me alone!" When I reached the gate, I turned back.

To my relief, the sweaty man had given up.

He was now on his knees, head in hands, clearly upset at the missed opportunity. Ivor, who'd been watching the show from the other side of the park, had vanished. I wasn't about to search for him.

My priority was to stagger home to Mum.

I wasn't in pain, but I still had that out-of-body sensation, and it terrified me. I've always thought this episode had the makings of a great song:

♫ *Is this the real life or just fantasy?*

Fell from a high slide, no escape from reality.

I opened my eyes, looked up to the skies and see…

I was a poor boy.

I needed surgery.

Because I easily fell, for letting go, From a little high, to a little low… Any sympathy the man showed, Didn't really matter to me.

Tooo meee! ♫

***

I eventually arrived home to an empty house. No parents.

In my panic, I remembered that our neighbour, Mrs Grey, worked at the local hospital. So I staggered to her door and knocked for help.

Mrs Grey: "Hello, Steven. What can I do for you?"

Without saying a word, I spun around, revealing my blood-soaked shirt. She instantly turned as grey as her name.

Mrs Grey: "What in God's name happened to you?"

Me: "I fell from the top of the slide and landed on my head. Mum and Dad aren't home, so I'm not sure what to do."

Mrs Grey: "Wait there while I get my coat. I'm taking you straight to the hospital." I'd forgotten Mrs Grey didn't have a car.

So off we went, on a twenty-minute walk to Barry Accident and Emergency Hospital. On the way, we passed the scene of the crime: Bassett Park.

My vision was still a little hazy for 'some unknown reason', but I thought I caught a glimpse of Ivor, still in the park.

Ming The Merciless and Puppies

We arrived at the hospital, and I was immediately taken into a doctor's office for a check-up. The doctor peeled off my shirt, which was glued to my skin with blood.

I prayed he wouldn't notice my blood-stained Y-fronts. I was in no state for a full Brazilian.

He draped a towel over my shoulders and began sponging away the blood to reveal the full extent of my sporting injury.

Doctor Sponge: "You need an X-ray." No way was I letting them operate on me.

As a well-educated seven-year-old, I thought an X-ray meant knives, stitches, and, worst of all, being knocked out.

Me *(shouting)*: "Nooooo! I don't want an operation, I want my Mummy!" Then I started crying hysterically.

Knocking me out?

Bassett Park tarmac couldn't do it, so no way was I letting the hospital try.

They tried to convince me that an X-ray was just like a normal camera taking a photo, except it shoots rays of light that pass harmlessly through your head to check for damage.

Shooting rays of light through my head?

I don't think so. I'd seen too many episodes of *Flash Gordon* fighting Ming the Merciless to believe ray guns were harmless.

By the time Mum and Dad arrived, the Radiologist, Ming the Merciless, had finished his shift, removing the threat of filling my head with X-rays.

The doctor spoke briefly to Mum.

Doctor Sponge: "Steven wouldn't allow us to give him an X-ray, but I've done a thorough examination. It looks like just a nasty gash. If he starts acting strange, bring him straight back."

Dad *(comedy mode activated)*: "Act strange? He's been strange all his life." Mum gave Dad a menacing stare.

Dad *(comedy mode deactivated)*: "OK, Doctor. Will do."

Thankfully, Dad had his Ford Zephyr, so I didn't have to walk home.

When we arrived, Ivor's mum came running down the street towards us.

Ivor's Mum: "Oh my God! Mrs Grey told me all about the slide incident. How are you, Steven?"

Mum: "He's OK. He has his Dad's hard head." Mum gave Dad another menacing stare.

Ivor's Mum: "That's good news. I'd better go, Ivor's just brought a cute puppy home."

I Bloody knew it!

Thanks to *Charley Says*, I'd avoided coming home with my own cute puppy.

And even more impressive, I'd single-handedly foiled Ming the Merciless from ray-gunning my head until my face glowed orange, making me look like Donald Trump's love child.

Believing

Onions and Phobias

In the 1960s, if you asked a seven-year-old whether they believed in God, most kids would say yes.

But not me.

And here's why.

Let's rewind to Holton Road School, sometime in the mid-sixties. I was in the Infant School, which was separated from the Junior School by a narrow concrete lane. On top of the Junior School lived the dreaded Senior Girls.

Yes, the dreaded 'Senior Girls'.

One day during class, I suddenly had the urgent need to visit the toilet, not the urinal, the other one.

With the teacher's permission, I set off across the playground, under the shelter, and up to the top of the yard where the boys' toilets were located.

Halfway to the boys' toilets, I spotted a pack of Senior Girls loitering menacingly near the entrance to the girls' loos. To reach my destination, I'd have to walk right past them.

I paused and considered the potential Clash:

♫ *Should I stay or should I go now? If I go there will be trouble…*

If I stay it will be double… ♫

The rumblings in my tummy gave me the answer. I had to go.

As I approached, two of the girls pointed at me and burst into giggles.

Maybe they'd clocked my undeniable good looks and decided to overlook the minor detail that I was six years younger than them.

I thought: "Play it cool, Steve. This could be their lucky day."

I stopped skipping and switched to my best John Wayne swagger. Big mistake.

Before I knew it, the two girls grabbed me and dragged me into the girls' toilets. Bloody hell, I thought. I'd overdone the John Wayne.

Two's a Crowd

They shoved me through a toilet cubicle door and slammed it shut behind me. And there I was, face to face with a girl mid-motion on the toilet.

She looked up, froze, her face a cocktail of panic and disbelief. A silent scream that said: "I didn't order room service."

We stared at each other in sheer horror, like two strangers trapped in a lift. Except one was actively pooing, and the other resisting the urge to make it a double act.

At this point, I had limited options:

   1. Formally introduce myself, no handshakes, obviously.

2.   Offer her a handful of greaseproof toilet paper.

3.   Scream loudly.

I wasn't sure of her options, but I think we both simultaneously chose Option 3:

SCREAM LOUDLY

I spun around and yanked at the door, desperate to escape both the embarrassment and the choking aroma.

But the two giggling girls outside were holding it shut, like prison wardens with a twisted sense of humour.

Between shouts of "Let me out! Let me out!" I gasped to my fellow occupant:

"FLUSH! FLUSH!"

The stench inside the cubicle was like bad pickled onions, so potent it made my lip curl and twitch like I was doing a poor Elvis Presley impression.

Eventually, the Evil Two succumbed to my desperate pleading (and audible heaving) and released the door.

I bolted for freedom and fresh air.

As I exited, I heard them shout after me: "Elvis has left the building!"

Faith, Fumes, and Fabric Fusion

That traumatic episode left a lasting mark. To this day, I have a phobia of public toilets, and the mere thought of pickled onions makes me dry heave.

Some months later, during class, I felt the familiar rumble.

But thanks to the Evil Two, my newly acquired toilet phobia left me no choice but to hold on until the home-time bell.

When it rang, I was off, out the gates and down the back lanes, taking the quickest route home. Unfortunately, running wasn't helping.

My long strides became shorter and shorter until I looked like I was competing in an Olympic walking race.

By the time I reached the top of Guys Road, two streets from home, I was moving like a member of Monty Python's 'Ministry of Silly Walks'.

At the bottom of the hill, with only 100 metres to go, things were not looking good. At this point, I was officially touching cloth.

I leant against a Morris Minor parked at the roadside for support and began emergency bum-cheek clenching exercises, a last-ditch attempt to reverse the false start.

Things seemed to settle.

So, looking skyward, I played my ace card.

Me *(whispering)*: "Please God! If you stop me pooing my pants, I'll believe in you forever."

And there it was, a seven-year-old boy, desperately asking God to prove His existence through emergency bowel intervention.

Then it happened.

A muffled voice from nowhere:

"WHAT DO YOU WANT?"

Me *(whispering in shock)*: "Is that you, Jesus's Dad?"

Suddenly, the window of the Morris Minor I was leaning against began to open. The source of the voice was revealed.

The muffled tone was replaced by a full-throated shriek as the male occupant wound the window down further.

Morris Minor Occupant *(shrieking)*: "Oi! What are you doing to my car?" I had no idea anyone was inside.

To say he frightened the shit out of me would be an understatement.

Me: "Nothing, sir! Nothing, honest!"

I was leaning against the driver's door, which meant he couldn't open it.

And by winding down the window, he'd unwittingly positioned himself in the direct path of my freshly deposited nugget.

I looked at his face.

His eyes began to glaze over from the effects of the pickled onion aroma.

Gasping for air, he frantically wound the window back up, just before the glass sealed him in.

Morris Minor Occupant: "Bugger off, kid! Go and lean on someone else's car!" I glanced back at him one last time.

His lip was curled and twitching.

He looked like a fellow Elvis impersonator.

I put on my best John Wayne swagger, not out of confidence, but necessity, and headed home to rid myself of my uninvited Y-fronts guest.

Mum greeted me at the front door.

Mum: "Hello, love. How was your day at schoooool… wait, what's that awful smell? Have you been eating pickled onions?"

Knowing I'd come home with more in my pants than when I'd left, and far too embarrassed to explain.

Me *(innocently lying)***:** "Yes."

Without waiting for a response, I dashed to the toilet for a quick decontamination. To my horror, the unwelcome visitor had fused with the fabric.

With limited options, I wrapped the whole mess, pants and all, in toilet paper, kebab-style.

Tucked the warm parcel under my jumper, snuck outside, and lobbed the evidence into our neighbour's bin.

Returned inside… to a pickled onion aroma–free zone. No evidence of my bowel betrayal.

Unfortunately, the kebab wrapping was my Wednesday undies, part of my days-of-the-week set. Which meant I was forced to endure a pants-free Wednesday for the rest of the term.

At seven years old, I became a 'Non-Believer'.

If there was a God, He'd well and truly let me down in my hour of need.

Now, whenever uninvited people of religion appear at my door to question my faith, I simply relay this tale and ask:

"Why do YOU think God let me poo my pants?"

They usually just curl their lip like Elvis… and quietly back away.

Steve Rowley

The Christmas Party

Fairies and Footballers

The Christmas parties at Holton Road Primary School were legendary. They were my second favourite time of the year.

My absolute favourite?

The last day before the summer holidays.

School, in general, was an activity I could've done without.

Although, to give credit where it's due, I did leave with extremely neat handwriting.

Why?

Because I spent hours copying my mum's handwriting so I could fraudulently write my own absentee notes.

To avoid being caught out by handwriting inconsistencies, I even rewrote genuine notes my mum gave me for school.

This allowed me to enjoy endless school-free days during my final years.

The result?

Unclassified exam results in both Physics and Chemistry. Catastrophic Fail.

Totally worth it.

Pantomime Time

The Christmas parties followed the same format every year:

• Bring food and pop.

• Eat and drink everyone else's food and pop.

• Wear a fancy-dress costume.

• Get paraded around every classroom so the entire school could admire your Christmas outfit.

For six years in a row, I wore my latest football kit. Yes! I dressed as a footballer.

As did the other fifteen boys in my class. The girls?

They dressed as fairies.

The parties always started with great excitement, until the boys began arguing about which football team was the 'Bestest'.

Meanwhile, Michelle would be crying to the teacher:

Michelle: "Miss! Karen poked me in the eye with her wand!" Or:

"Miss! Karen's being mean to me!"

I always wondered why the fairy victims didn't just cast a spell on the perpetrators. Turn them into frogs or something.

But remember, we were in the 1970s. We were old-fashioned.

Apart from teachers, there were only boys and girls in the classroom. Frogs were definitely not allowed.

Unless, of course, it was Christmas party time. Then all bets were off.

Sometimes I wonder what a modern-day Christmas party looks like. Boys in tutus, arguing over whose fairy wand has the most power.

Karens still causing havoc, well, some things never change.

Festive Fashion Face-Off

The party would be in full swing when our teacher, Miss Lewis, clapped her hands to get our attention.

Miss Lewis: "Right, children, follow me. It's time to show off your costumes!"

And just like lemmings, we trailed behind her, out of the classroom, down the corridor, toward the next class.

We stood in silence, listening to the laughter and shouting from the party already in full swing on the other side of the door.

Then came the secret teacher's knock:

Ra-ta-ta-ta.

Inside, Mrs Clutten, ever vigilant, immediately clapped her hands.

Mrs Clutten: "Children, children! Quiet, please!"

The class fell silent.

Ra-ta-ta-ta.

Mrs Clutten *(theatrically)*: "Who can that be at the door?"

Cue Miss Lewis, opening the door and marching her Christmas display team to the front of the classroom.

She instructed us to shuffle closer and closer together until we were crammed into a line, posing sideways like contestants in a Miss World competition.

Except that, instead of porcelain smiles, we wore expressions of pure awkwardness.

We stood there, face to face with another class of fairies and footballers, like two tribes in a standoff.

Mrs Clutten *(enthusiastically)*: "Miss Lewis has brought her class to show you their wonderful Christmas costumes!"

She slowly worked her way along the line, stopping at each Miss World contestant.

Mrs Clutten: "And what are you dressed as today?"

The answers came like a broken record:

- "A fairy."
- "A fairy."
- "Croak…"
- "A footballer."
- "A footballer."

And so it went, until every child had declared their status.

Then, to the relief of Mrs Clutten's footballers and fairies, we were marched out to continue our school-wide tour of awkwardness.

After visiting every class and presenting ourselves to hundreds of other fairies and footballers, we returned to our classroom to resume the party.

We had barely restarted the fun when,

Ra-ta-ta-ta

Another bloody secret teacher's knock.

Miss Lewis *(claps hands)*: "Children, children, quiet please.

Ra-ta-ta-ta

Miss Lewis *(theatrically)*: "Who can that be at the door?"

Interlude:

I'm convinced pantomiming is part of teacher training.

And I can already hear teachers reading this, shouting:

"Oh no, it's NOT!"

To which I say:

"Oh yes, it is!"

I rest my case.

Outerlude:

Where was I…?

Back to the *Ra-ta-ta-ta*.

The classroom would go from mayhem to silence in an instant.

Then, to our utter astonishment, we were presented with a line of, you'll never believe it, fairies, frogs, and footballers.

They stood there like a police ID parade.

I wanted to shout: "It's the Arsenal goalkeeper! He stole the Oxo-flavoured crisps from the tuck shop!"

Then came the ritual roll call:

"A fairy. A fairy. Croak. Croak. A footballer. A footballer."

Obviously, there were two Karens in that class.

The stop-start party continued for the rest of the day.

The boys, having consumed too many blue Smarties, transformed from footballers into acrobatic aeroplanes, dive-bombing the fairies at breakneck speed.

The fairies, wanting to eat their fairy cakes in peace, retaliated.

With a swish of their wands, they turned the acrobatic aeroplanes into pink leotard ballerinas.

Wine O'Clock

The teachers, utterly exhausted and emotionally drained, had their prayers answered when the home-time bell rang.

They sent us on our way with an imaginary kick up the bum, wishing us a Merry Christmas and a long, long break.

I can picture them now at their desks, feet up, wine in hand, blue Smarties melting in their palms.

And there they remained…

Until the first child of the new term knocked on the door with a *Ra-ta-ta-ta.*

Noddy Holder is Coming to Town

Christmas morning in our house began at 1:30 am, with my extremely excited mum bursting into my bedroom.

Mum: "It's Christmas! Wake up, Father Christmas has been! Quick, come downstairs and see what he's left you!"

Me: "For God's sake, Mum, I'm bloody 35 years old." Hang on… I've jumped too far forward.

Let's rewind to Christmas 1973, when I was 10 years old.

Mum: "It's Christmas! Wake up, wake up!"

"Father Christmas has been! Quick, come downstairs and see what he's left you!"

Her voice at that time in the morning sounded like I was stuck in a telephone box with Noddy Holder, mid-yodel, every syllable of "IT'S CHRISTMAS!" ricocheting off the glass like a glam-rock alarm clock.

I was instantly jolted awake from a bad dream.

Me *(shouting)*: "Mayday! Mayday! We're going to crash!"

The blue Smarties and acrobatic planes were still doing laps in my subconscious.

Mum *(gently)*: "Steve, it's okay. You're just having a bad dream. Mum's here."

Me: "Sorry, Mum."

Mum: "That's alright! Now get up, Father Christmas has been!"

Then the Noddy Holder tribute act disappeared into my sister's room to deliver the same wake-up call.

Christmas was Mum's favourite time of year.

She loved nothing more than watching our faces light up as we opened our presents.

Okay… this year was slightly different.

The Wrong Team

I sat surrounded by wrapped presents from Father Christmas and opened the first one:

Adidas football boots.

Me *(excitement level 1)*: "YES!"

Next: white football socks.

Me *(excitement level 2)*: "YES! YES!" I was convinced I knew what was coming next.

Third present: blue football shorts.

Me *(confused)*: "Oh…"

Fourth present: a blue Chelsea football top.

Me *(disappointment level 1)*: "NOOOOO!"

Mum *(concerned)*: "What's wrong?"

Let me clarify: at the time, I was obsessed with Leeds United.

That year, they were top of the league, and my dream was to have their latest kit:

White socks. WHITE shorts. WHITE top.

Being ten, I couldn't contain my disappointment, even on Christmas morning.

Me *(disappointment level 10)*: "I'm a Leeds United supporter and I hate Chelsea!"

I kicked the sofa in temper.

I considered kicking my older sister, who was smirking at me, but didn't fancy spending Christmas morning in Accident and Emergency, having a football boot removed from my rectum.

Mum was disappointed and upset all at once.

Mum *(teary)*: "You are so ungrateful! Some children are waking up this morning to NO PRESENTS! You don't know how lucky you are!"

Then:

"That football kit cost Mum and Dad a lot of money! And we got it because it was on offer, and the money we saved bought you Kerplunk! And now I've gone and spoiled that surprise too!"

Wait a minute… Mum and Dad bought the presents?

Clearly a cover-up for Father Christmas's cock-up.

Mum disappeared into the kitchen in floods of tears.

Dad followed, but not before performing his infamous silent shouting routine.

He mouthed angry words at me in silence, punctuated by sharp nods of the head.

Dad *(nodding)*: "….."

Then he vanished into the kitchen.

Moments later, his head reappeared for an encore glare and silent shout.

Dad *(nodding loudly)*: "….."

To this day, I have no idea what he said.

Maybe it was a warning not to kick my sister, who was still smirking and cuddling her presents like a smug elf.

The situation calmed down when Dad convinced me that if I wore the Chelsea top inside out, it would look like a Cardiff City kit, my second favourite team.

After a couple of games of Kerplunk, Christmas Day was back on track.

With dinner done and dusted, we collapsed in front of the telly for the Top of the Pops Christmas Special.

Glam rock was king. Noddy Holder was screaming. And Mum was still smiling.

Twinkle Twinkle I'm The Star

Every group on Top of the Pops wore silver or gold sparkling costumes, making them look like the coolest people on the planet.

As I watched my favourite pop stars in full flow, a defining moment occurred.

Why dress as a footballer for next year's Christmas party… when I could dress as a 'Glam Rock Superstar'?

I imagined myself standing in the display line, surrounded by fairies and footballers.

Mrs Clutten *(dramatically)*: "And what are you dressed as today?"

Fairy. Fairy. Croak. Footballer. Footballer.

Then, my turn.

One step forward. Chest out.

Me: "Today, Mrs Clutten, I am a Glam Rock Superstar."

The acrobatic aeroplanes would crash to the floor.

The fairies would scream with excitement, desperate for a love chat with me.

There might be a croak or two, but I'd ignore them.

Decision made.

One Year Later - The Birth of Twinkle

It was the day before the Christmas Party and my first attempt at tailoring.

Planning was critical.

My materials:

• One old cowboy shirt

• A pair of flared jeans

• Platform shoes

• A box of aluminium foil

• Sticky tape

• A tube of glue

• And a bucket full of enthusiasm

My mission: to magically transform these ingredients into Twinkle, 'The Glam-Rockiest Costume' Holton Road Primary School had ever seen.

I worked in secret behind a locked door in the spare bedroom.

Rolled out aluminium cooking foil.

Spread glue.

Pressed the back of the shirt onto the foil.

Let it dry.

Repeated on the front.

With seamstress-like skill, I cut the foil around the arms and buttons, slid it onto a hanger, and hid it in the wardrobe.

Then came the jeans.

Disaster struck, the glue cap came off.

Glue everywhere.

Then, a knock at the door?

Dad: "Why is the door locked? Open it now!"

The game was up. I'd have to reveal Twinkle prematurely.

Me: "Hang on, Dad, I've had a bit of an accident. Sticky stuff all over my hands and jeans. I'm just cleaning it up with a tissue."

There was a pregnant pause.

Dad *(stuttering)***:** "Uhm… don't worry! We'll chat later."

He disappeared, muttering something about glasses and bad eyesight.

Crisis averted.

Then I continued cleaning up the mess.

Soon, my flared jeans were completely covered in aluminium foil.

Not sure how to hang them up, I laid them on the bed and gently covered them with a blanket.

Moments later, using my cobbler-like wizardry, I became the proud owner of a pair of aluminium-covered platform shoes, hidden under the bed like precious contraband.

Twinkle was complete!

Super impressed with myself, I unlocked the door and skipped downstairs, feeling like Yves Saint Laurent on the eve of his first fashion show.

The Reveal

The morning of the Christmas party had arrived.

Bursting with excitement, I jumped out of bed and ran into the spare bedroom.

I peeked under the blanket and into the wardrobe, everything was exactly as I'd left it.

The Floating Frog

Mum shouted before she and Dad left for work:

Mum: "Your Rola Cola and Marshmallow Snowballs for your Christmas party are on the kitchen table."

Now I just needed my sister to leave for school.

Not a problem.

Five minutes later, she was gone.

Then it was just me and Twinkle, home alone.

A year in the making, and the moment was finally here. Buzzing with anticipation, I entered the spare bedroom.

I removed the blanket covering my silver jeans, pulled the silver platform shoes from under the bed, and lifted my silver shirt from the wardrobe.

I laid it out, Twinkle in full, shimmering glory.

As I stood there, the biggest smirk I could fit on my face appeared.

I briefly compared myself to:

Clark Kent, mid-transformation into Superman. Then that woman, spinning into Wonder Woman… then Michael Palin, becoming Bicycle Repair Man.

Now it was my turn to become my own superhero:

'Twinkle Boy, the Glam Rock Superstar'.

I sat on the edge of the bed and gently pulled on my silver jeans.

A few bits of Sellotape came undone, but I pressed them back into place.

Putting on the silver platform shoes was a breeze.

Then magic happened, I slid into my silver shirt.

Twinkle and I became one.

I looked at myself in the wardrobe mirror and stumbled back in amazement.

Oh my God. A Twinkle star was born.

I stood there, staring at our reflection.

My imagination went into overdrive.

I pictured myself strutting to school along the busiest road in town.

Everyone was looking:

Mothers pushing prams, grandmothers with grandchildren, old men with newspapers under their arms.

All pointing as I strutted past.

All commenting:

"Look at that silly twat."

Undeterred, the only vision I cared about was walking into Mrs Clutten's classroom.

And that moment she'd ask,

"And what are you dressed as today?"

Foiled

Meanwhile, back in the spare bedroom, my shot at Holton Road Primary School cult status was suddenly, literally, ripped away from me.

It was time to leave our reflection in the mirror as destiny called.

I took two strides toward the door,

'RIIIIIP'.

The sound of aluminium foil tearing echoed like a death knell.

At that moment, I discovered aluminium foil is not the go-to material for tailoring.

Patches of foil hung from me as I turned to face the mirror.

But this time, it looked like Twinkle had lost a battle with Edward Scissorhands.

Broken-hearted, with tears in my eyes, Twinkle and I parted company.

I gathered the shredded foil from my shirt and jeans and threw the evidence in the bin, a final act of damage control to avoid further embarrassment.

Three Frogs in a Fountain

There I stood, in the line in front of Mrs Clutten's class.

Mrs Clutten: "And what are you dressed as today?"

Me *(defeated)***:** "A footballer."

Then a voice from the other class: "Why is the Chelsea striker wearing silver platform shoes?"

The class erupted into laughter.

Everyone pointed at me.

I'd forgotten to turn my shirt inside out. And in my emotional state, I'd also forgotten to remove the aluminium foil from my platform shoes.

Standing next to me was Michelle the fairy.

In desperation, I whispered:

Me: "If you turn me into a frog, I'll give you my Marshmallow Snowballs."

Wish granted.

I spent the rest of the day sitting under the fountain in the school fishpond with two Karens,

'Three Frogs in a Fountain'.

And there we stayed, croaking until the home-time bell rang and broke the fairy spell.

Twinkle was gone. But the legend of the silver shoes lived on.

Steve Rowley

Pea Shooterist

Mission Improbable

Always looking for something new to entertain ourselves, Pete, a few of the lads, and I bought some peashooters, along with a couple of rounds of ammunition: boxes of Leo's Dried Peas.

So there we were, overactive twelve-year-old boys, armed with peashooters.

What could possibly go wrong?

The day started with, "Who can shoot the six cans off the wall the quickest?"

That held our attention for about an hour… before the tin cans were replaced by overactive twelve-year-old targets.

Like any major conflict, it was only a matter of time before things escalated into an all-out battle, shooting at each other in a full-blown free-for-all.

I'm not suggesting, even for a minute, that World War II began with Winston Churchill and Hitler blowing dry peas at each other…but it felt close.

Interlude:

These People Walk Amongst Us

I once rented a field from a proper gentleman, Mr Davies, known to some as Major Davies.

During a special operation in World War II, he and his unit were on the Normandy beaches the night before the D-Day landings, laying communication cables in the sand for the invasion, right under the noses of the Germans.

No fuss. No fanfare.

Just quiet courage.

Outerlude:

Where was I?…

Twelve-year-old targets

With ammunition running low, we started reusing peas from the ground.

Here's a handy hint for all would-be pea-shooterists:

Only use a dry pea once in battle.

Apart from spreading diseases, mushy peas will clog your barrel, rendering your weapon useless.

A very impotent lesson.

Having successfully negotiated a ceasefire, I suggested we needed a new target, something that would unite us all once again.

A war committee was formed, and over a bottle of dandelion and burdock pop and a couple of Curly Wurly chocolate bars, it was decided:

Due to the damaging effects of carbon dioxide emissions on the environment…

A war on motor cars was declared.

We needed a name for our newly formed unit to carry out the mission.

Eventually, we all agreed on a name: 'The Welsh Artillery Northern Kombat Elite Regiment'.

Or, as we liked to call ourselves… 'The WANKERs'.

We were going to launch a national radio campaign to inform the people of Wales of our intentions…

But the local grocery shop was about to close, and we needed more ammunition.

Ambush and Peas

So, under the cover of darkness, armed with pea shooters and an extra-large box of Leo's dried peas, we headed to Gladstone Park for our first special 'seek-and-annoy' mission.

The park sat next to a main road, separated by a stone balustrade.

Road on one side. Bushes on the other, ideal for launching a surprise attack without being seen.

We set up camp in the bushes.

Locked and loaded, we pushed our pea shooters through the balustrade and patiently waited for the enemy to fall into our ambush.

As cars innocently drove past, we took aim at their wheels and, without notice, fired dried peas at will.

We were having great success… until the moment I was about to fire another round, Jeremy whispered, loudly:

Jeremy: "Look! Look! There's a guy running this way!"

The shock made me suck instead of blow, instantly lodging a dried pea in the back of my throat.

My eyes watered as I tried not to cough.

Before we knew it, the driver of one of our targets, henceforth known as 'Field Marshal Willie Schnapper, Commander of the German Panzer Division', was more or less standing directly above us.

Thanks to the street lighting, we could see him clearly on his side of the balustrade.

Luckily, he couldn't see us crouched in the shadowed undergrowth just beneath him.

It was rapidly turning into a scene from Dad's Army.

Willie Schnapper *(shouting)*: "Vee know you are in dar! Come out with your peeing shooters up, you Velsh shaggers of da sheep! You vill not escape capture!"

Christ. He'd just declared war.

Then, out of nowhere, Willie Schnapper produced a cigarette lighter.

With one flick, he transformed it into a miniature flamethrower, lighting up the immediate area in his search for us.

Fortunately, the rhododendrons still concealed our position.

Willie Schnapper waved his flame about like a deranged concertgoer, it looked like a Robbie Williams concert.

I think he was hoping the mesmerising waving of flame would cause us to start singing Angels, revealing our location.

Bloody crafty Germans!

Resisting the urge to sing, we urgently needed an escape plan.

Still choking on the dried pea, I decided to take charge.

Since speaking risked detection, I launched into a full sign-language routine.

Having never studied sign language at school, I unearthed a skill I had no idea I possessed.

Without hesitation, I began coordinating the escape.

• I pointed to Paul and Jeremy.

• Turned the pointing action into a peace sign: You two.

• Flipped the peace sign and moved my hand up and down a few times: 'Go quickly'.

• Finished with an arcing motion to the left-hand exit of the park: Your escape route.

They both nodded.

Mission understood.

Next, I used the same technique for Colin and Brian, the conjoined twins, to exit via the right-hand side.

Instead of nodding, Colin used his own hand signals, pointing to himself, then Brian, then shrugging.

He was basically asking if I meant one or both of them to exit right.

Using my inherited angrily mouthed silent-words technique, I confirmed:

YES, both of you!

Then I gave them two additional aggressive 'go quickly' gestures.

I turned to Pete, who was beside me, and indicated we'd exit via the rear of the park.

Just then, Field Marshal Willie Schnapper became distracted by a swarm of moths drawn to his flamethrower.

Perfect moment.

I gave the big thumbs-up.

The WANKERs, pea shooters in hand, leapt to their feet and, like trained operatives, scarpered in different directions.

The rustling of bushes caught Schnapper's attention.

He paused his newly acquired moth fetish:

Willie Schnapper *(commanding)*: "HALT! You Vankers!"

You Wankers?

How did he know the name of our top-secret regiment? There must be a mole in our regiment.

Pete and I headed for the rear exit. I turned back to check on the others.

Paul and Jeremy had made it through the left-side exit.

Meanwhile, Colin and Brian were attempting to run in opposite directions, a logistical nightmare.

Once Pete and I had successfully exited, I glanced back.

Field Marshal Willie Schnapper still stood above our abandoned camp, now like the Statue of Liberty, luring even more moths with his flame, and humming *Angels* to himself.

Operation Stealth

With the threat of being caught, and the looming possibility of an SS-style interrogation by Mum and Dad, Pete and I took no chances. Operation Stealth was a go.

We zigzagged through the suburban backstreets, taking so many twists and turns that even a bloodhound with a sat-nav would've struggled to keep pace.

After two and a half hours of covert manoeuvres, calculated detours, and one near-miss involving a hedge suspiciously shaped like a policeman, we were finally reunited with our regiment.

HQ: Jeremy's garage.

Just five minutes from Gladstone Park, assuming you weren't being pursued by a flame-wielding Field Marshal with moth-control issues.

Debriefed

Paul and Jeremy were thrilled to see us, assuming we'd been captured and were being held at Butlitz, also known locally as Barry Island Butlins Holiday Park.

Then I noticed Colin standing sideways, alone, with a disappointed look on his face.

Me *(shocked)*: "My God! Where's Brian?"

Paul: "Colin lost contact with Brian just outside the park."

That was enough for me.

I instantly knew who the mole was.

We had to act fast, before Willie Schnapper and that traitor Brian launched a counter-offensive.

Just as I prepared to call it in…

Brian's head popped out from behind Colin.

Brian *(jokingly)*: "Ha ha! Fooled you!" Everyone fell about laughing, including me.

Colin and Brian were always pulling stunts.

They were proper comedians.

I often said they should form a double act.

I even came up with a catchphrase:

"From me. To you."

Eventually, their careers moved them away from the area and, sadly, we lost contact.

Even now, I wonder if they're still working together?

Back at HQ, we held a debriefing.

Jeremy informed us the German Tank Commander had driven past three times before parking his 'tank' and sprinting toward our dugout.

Although the mission was successful, it was decided to disband the 'WANKERs', not in fear of Field Marshal Schnapper, but in fear of someone far more dangerous…

Our Commander-in-Chiefs, alias: Mums and Dads.

We all stood in a circle, peashooters raised high, and toasted:

"TO THE WANKERs!"

And that was it.

The end of an era.

A touching moment.

We all reached for tissues, some for tears, some not.

The SAS has its motto: "Who Dares Wins."

But the WANKERs' motto: "Nobody Sees Us Coming."

Ahh… great memories.

Great mates.

And one hell of a Pea War.

Steve Rowley

Bogeying

The Great Pram Robbery

Every great bogey cart starts with two key components:

• A plank of wood

• And old pram wheels

Pete and I hadn't planned on building one, until fate handed us a shopping trolley of mischief.

Down a quiet lane, tucked beside a house, stood an abandoned pram.

Without exchanging a word, we looked at each other, then looked around.

Nobody in sight.

That confirmed it - *Abandoned.*

We stripped the shopping bags off the handles and gently lifted out a sleeping baby, delicately placing her on the nearest privet hedge without waking her.

Now, I know what you're thinking.

How did we know it was a girl?

Easy, the blanket was pink, and it was the '70s.

The other baby had a blue one.

Case closed.

So, with both babies resting peacefully on the hedge, we grabbed our newly acquired pram and bolted.

We barely made it around the corner when the shouts started:

"They've got our pram, GET 'EM!"

I turned to Pete.

"Don't look! Let's pretend they're not shouting at us."

I sneaked a peek, careful not to reveal my identity.

Behind us: a full-on *Rocky II*–style scene, the mob chasing Rocky, then jumping up and down, cheering as he raised his arms in the air. Iconic.

Not so iconic for us.

We were being pursued by an angry mob of youths, and one lady, breast out, expressing milk like a water cannon.

There would be no cheering if they caught us.

Me: "Pete! Let's see how fast this thing goes!"

We bolted, Silver Cross Formula One mode activated.

Adrenaline overruled logic.

Why we didn't just abandon the pram, and the remaining triplet, I have no idea.

After losing our pursuers, we became pram fugitives, sneaking through back lanes, whispering, "Go! Go! Go!" like low-budget spies.

Eventually, we made it to HQ, my shed, with the loot intact.

Well… almost.

Mrs Barnacle from number 25 intercepted us.

Mrs Barnacle: "Oh, is this your baby brother or sister?"

Me *(panicking)***:** "Not sure."

The baby was wrapped in a neutral yellow blanket.

Gender reveal: *Inconclusive.*

We handed her the baby and legged it.

Bogeytime: The Launch, The Limp, The Escape

Bogey Cart Assembly

We removed the wheels and dumped the frame in a nearby skip.

Next, the plank.

Easy.

It had been leaning against the shed for months.

I remembered it well, because I'd once jumped off the shed roof and landed on it… impaling my foot on a rusty nail.

It went straight through my shoe and lodged in the sole of my right foot.

I limped away on one firmly attached ski, desperately seeking Dad and his trusty claw hammer.

Mum did her mum thing:

Boiling water.

Epsom salts.

Concerned commentary.

Then Dad arrived, presenting the offending nail like an archaeologist.

Mum: "This is beyond Epsom salts. You need a tetanus injection."

Over the years, I've had more tetanus needles put in me than Luke Littler has darts in a treble twenty.

Silvercross Bogey Team

We built Bogey with additional accessories, wooden axles, screws, rope, bolts and washers.

Bogey assembled, it was 'Bogeytime'.

Pete, naturally, took the driver's seat.

He steered with rope tied to the front axle.

I was the engine, sitting back-to-back with Pete, propelling us forward with my feet along the straights.

Downhill? I spun around for turbo mode.

Once, we made it all the way to Barry Island, an hour's journey from home.

After bogeying along the promenade like seaside celebrities, we realised time was up and we needed to head home to check in with Mum.

Shortcut needed.

Across the docks.

There's a very steep hill from Barry Island down to the docks, called Battery Hill.

We pointed Bogey downhill, both of us facing forward, using our feet as brakes like bargain-bin Fred Flintstones.

Halfway down, we paused for a team huddle.

We calculated that our momentum, by the time we reached the bottom, wouldn't be strong enough to launch us into the docks, fifty metres away along flat ground.

A bold theory, considering we'd just failed our physics exam.

Also, a small oversight: I couldn't swim.

So getting it wrong wouldn't just mean a soggy landing, it would mean certain death for me.

Without fear or intelligence, I shouted, "Go!"

Bogey instantly turned into Thunderbird 9, hurtling down Battery Hill at breakneck speed.

Pete suddenly began to shake uncontrollably.

I knew this wasn't a good sign.

Pete *(panicking)*: "Speed wobble! Speed wobble! I can't control it!"

We veered left. Then right.

Still accelerating.

Just as I was about to shout, "Mummy!", a miracle occurred.

At the bottom of the hill stood a car, a small blue Hillman Imp.

It nobly sacrificed one side of its panelwork to bring Bogey to a shuddering stop.

We bounced hard into its side.

Bogey survived. We survived.

We… staggered.

Shaken but not stirred, we checked our limbs.

Just then, some workers, ten metres away from the undamaged side of the car, painting palm trees on the docks café, paused mid-stroke. One of them called out:

Palm Artist: "Hope you guys have insurance!"

Pete *(innocently)*: "What's insurance?"

The Palm Artist examined Bogey from a distance, still somehow intact.

Palm Artist *(jokingly)*: "I think your vehicle's probably worth more than my car!"

The Floating Frog

The other workers erupted into laughter.

I saw the damage inflicted on the poor Hillman Imp, it wasn't good.

The Palm Artist, blissfully unaware, was shielded by the good side of the car.

Time to scarper.

I activated my theatrical dramatics:

Me: "Aagh! My leg! I think it's broken, we have to go!"

I dragged Bogey towards the lock gates, limping like Laurence Olivier in a school nativity.

Meanwhile, Pete was deep in financial philosophy.

Pete *(curiously)*: "So how do I get this insurance thing?"

I ramped up the drama to Oscar-worthy levels.

Me *(dramatically)*: "Pete! I can't feel my foot! We need to go, like NOW!"

Still distracted…

Pete: "But what about the insurance thing? I'm genuinely interested."

Through gritted teeth, I gave him the Rowley crash course.

"He wants your pocket money for the next year to fix the car!"

Penny dropped.

Pete turned into Usain Bolt, breaking the lock gate crossing speed record.

I spun around and chased after him.

In the confusion, I'd forgotten which leg I'd supposedly broken, so I ran like both were in callipers, Forrest Gump style.

Out of sight, Usain reverted to Pete, waiting patiently.

Pete: "Why are you running like you've shit yourself?"

My acting was so convincing, even I believed my legs were broken.

Me: "Never mind, let's just get out of here."

We hopped onto Bogey and headed home.

Most of the journey was spent explaining insurance policies, Third Party Fire & Theft versus Full Comprehensive, with all the clarity of someone who'd just crashed a pram into a Hillman.

The Dukes of Hazardous Decisions

The final stretch of our journey home took us down a footpath between houses.

Downhill start.

Sweeping left turn.

Flat section to slow up.

Grassy slope on the side of the footpath.

We'd done it dozens of times before.

And we knew… that stretch at the bottom of the path was long enough to stop Bogey safely, before the road.

As long as no new variables appeared.

So what could possibly go wrong?

Well… let me tell you.

At the top of the footpath, Pete and I, facing forward and full of misplaced confidence, invited Bogey to do its worst.

We accelerated quickly, and by the time we hit the sweeping bend, we'd reached Mach 1, on a chassis made of a plank and a prayer.

We rounded the bend beautifully and hit the flat section, expecting a graceful stop.

That's when the elderly gentleman and his corgi appeared dead ahead.

"Houston, we have a problem."

Both Pete and I screamed:

"GET OUT OF THE WAY!"

I waved frantically, desperately signalling danger.

He waved back cheerfully, mistaking it for a friendly hello.

Pete had a decision to make:

A) Turn Bogey into a three-man bobsleigh with an onboard furry mascot

B) Steer us down a steep grassy embankment and into the arms of fate

Thanks to Pete's freshly acquired grasp of insurance policies, he went with Option B, preserving his no-claims bonus and yanking Bogey violently to the right.

Bogey responded like an extra from *The Dukes of Hazzard*, launching into a sideways somersault that would've made Bo and Luke proud.

We tumbled down the embankment in a chaotic carousel of grass–sky–grass–sky–brambles, gripping whatever part of Bogey wasn't spinning or stabbing us.

We crash-landed in a bramble bush, limbs twisted into a pose straight out of *Twister: Contortionist Edition*.

Bogey lay on its side, two wheels still in the air, defiantly spinning, a portrait of mechanical carnage.

Eventually, we untangled ourselves, pausing to check our limbs and pride were still vaguely intact.

We waved back at the still-smiling gentleman, then dragged Bogey back to the path.

Pete: "Bogey looks OK to me."

Me: "Yep. Let's go."

Back in the driver's seat.

Pit stop at my house for a quick debrief with Mum.

Then off to Pete's.

Now here's an important lesson:

Insurance includes a free structural assessment of damaged vehicles.

Had we called a provider, they'd have sent someone to check Bogey's frame integrity and strongly recommended we stop riding around recklessly, thus putting an end to these silly stunts.

No time for insurance claims.

We took a shortcut to Pete's and paused at the top of a gravelly lane.

Both facing forward.

Confident.

We set off.

Bogey picked up speed… then started wobbling unnaturally.

I gripped the plank tightly, for dear life, before all hell broke loose.

The rear axle fell off, causing the plank to slam down.

Well, not quite onto the gravel.

Onto my fingers.

Which, of course, were underneath the plank, where I was holding on for grim life.

And to add to the situation… I was sitting on top of them, full body weight.

What followed was an eternity of fingers being dragged across gravel, skin and bone acting as brake pads.

When Bogey finally stopped, I stood up, freed my hands, and surveyed the damage.

Pete turned, laughing, until I held up my fingers.

Pete: "Shit. I can see bone."

Me: "I think I'd better get home."

Teenage Boys Don't Cry

Wrong.

I staggered home, holding my shredded hands like fragile chicken fillet skins.

Mum assessed my injury.

Mum: "Oh dear! That looks nasty. What are the black bits?"

Me: "Gravel."

Mum: "We'll need boiling water and Epsom salts."

She returned with a cauldron of lava, casually described as healing liquid.

Mum: "Don't be a baby, hands in."

For one glorious second… it felt cold.

Then my nerve endings phoned ahead.

"Molten hellfire incoming."

My lips tried to scream.

My lungs vetoed it.

If pain had subtitles, mine would've been fluent in seventeen languages.

Then came the scrubbing brush, like a medieval torture device disguised as hygiene.

Gravel extraction began.

By the time Pete arrived, I looked like someone who'd just watched the end of *Lassie: The Movie*.

Cry-sniffing.

Bloodshot eyes.

Holding it together like a soggy tissue.

Pete: "I've got bad news. I think Bogey is broken for good."

Great. Forget my degloved fingers, let's hold a memorial for a bloody go-kart.

I briefly considered slapping him with whatever skin was still hanging on.

Our Bogeying days had come to an abrupt end.

I'd tried convincing Karma the Triplets were fictional.

But Karma listens to local gossip, carries grudges, and has impeccable timing, and apparently… a wicked sense of humour.

Conkering

It's A Knockout

It was conker season, and word had spread around school that the Holy Grail of conkers could be found at Grange Park in Wenvoe Village, a thirty-minute bike ride from town.

According to local folklore, Wenvoe conkers were made of granite, and lightning would occur if two of them collided.

Actually, I think one of the boys just said the conkers were big and there were lots of them.

Either way, we were sold.

So a few lads from Mr Jones's class and I set off on our bikes for the four-mile pilgrimage in search of these legendary conkers.

When we arrived at Grange Park, we were surrounded by towering conker trees, Horse Chestnut trees to the well-educated.

Giant green, spiky balls, like nature's own virus emojis, dangled from every branch, swaying gently in the breeze.

Unable to contain our excitement, we immediately activated 'Operation Family Jewels'.

We dropped our bikes on the grass and went in search of COVID removal tools, also known as sticks.

Fully armed, we launched our offensive.

At one stage, we looked like deranged Morris dancers, sticks flying in every direction.

I briefly considered ringing the bell on my bike, just to complete the choreography.

Conkers rained from heaven.

Within the hour, we'd eradicated Wenvoe of the pandemic.

Our next task was to delicately open the spiky protective shells and reveal the shiny brown treasure hidden inside.

Using our COVID removal tools, we whacked the hell out of them until the shells spat their conkers out.

Mission accomplished.

The Expandables

We stood in a circle, admiring our stockpile of spoils.

Then reality kicked in.

We'd failed to involve a female in the planning of our expedition, which meant, inevitably, we'd overlooked the small but crucial matter of how to get the conkers home.

Everyone was wearing football shirts and jeans.

No coats.

No bags.

Carrying capacity: bugger all.

Well, everyone except one.

He was wearing baggy tracksuit bottoms.

I looked down and watched my 'Woolworth Windfield Wonder' tracksuit bottoms change shape as the boys crammed more and more conkers into my ever-expanding pockets.

By the time the last conker was onboard, my trousers resembled a costume from the popular British show *It's a Knockout*.

I couldn't bend my legs properly.

I waddled like a duck towards my bike.

Now, I'd always complained about my parents buying me a girly step-through bike.

But today?

It was the best bike in the world.

With no crossbar to navigate, I managed to mount the saddle.

Then, with circus clown–like grace, I began to pedal, zigzagging violently as I struggled to build momentum.

My performance had not gone unnoticed.

A small group of local lads at the far end of the park were pointing.

Others began to join them.

They weren't there for the 'circus candyfloss', that's for sure.

We sensed trouble and did what any self-respecting cycle-raiding party would do: we scarpered.

All the lads grabbed their bikes and took off at full speed.

As the pack disappeared into the distance, I suddenly realised my position: the slowest rider, trailing behind like a sacrificial 'Conker Mule' in case the Wenvoe locals gave chase.

I pedalled for my life, as if my nuts depended on it.

The more I tried to catch up, the more I resembled an overzealous member of Great Britain's *It's a Knockout* team.

But comical or not, my technique worked.

Eventually, I crossed the Barry border, breathless but triumphant.

Home turf.

Safe haven.

I felt a flash of pride.

Relief.

And a strange urge to hug my bike and whisper:

"Thanks for not throwing me to the Wenvoe Conker Retrieval Gang…

And for keeping my nuts exactly where nature intended."

Conkers and Consequences

By the time I got back to Maes-Y-Cwm Street HQ (also known as Jeremy's dad's garage), I was totally knackered.

The boys greeted me with: "You made it then?"

Then, without hesitation, or concern for my well-being, they descended like a pack of squirrels, grabbing handfuls of conkers from my pockets and unleashing a tsunami of shiny brown missiles across the garage floor.

My 'Conker Mule' status had been well and truly confirmed.

I stood there, traumatised, watching the sea of conkers roll across the concrete before settling into neat little piles, ready for distribution.

Before I could join the great conker auction, I felt something sharp digging into my leg.

I reached into my nearly empty pocket to investigate… and instantly yanked my hand back with a loud, involuntary girlie screech.

Some absolute bastard had shoved an unopened conker shell into my pocket.

One of its medieval torture spikes had embedded itself deep into my finger before snapping off, leaving me with the splinter from hell.

In agony and unable to extract it with my fingernails, I did what any wounded soldier would do:

I went in search of 'Nurse Mum'.

Feeling only mildly sorry for her little casualty, Mum began gouging at my finger with a sterilised needle, her sympathy levels plummeting after discovering I'd gone to Wenvoe without telling her.

Oops!

With the spike finally removed and my hand now throbbing from a twenty-minute soak in lava-hot Epsom salts, I returned to HQ to claim my rightful share of the loot.

Pete and Jeremy greeted me with an old plastic ice cream container.

Pete: "We shared them out evenly. These are yours."

I looked inside.

The contents resembled melted Maltesers more than championship conkers.

Me: "Why have I got all the small ones?"

Pete: "No, no! They were all shared out equally."

Me: "There were bigger ones than these. I still have the indentations in my thighs to prove it."

To rub even more Epsom salts into the wound, they'd placed the very shell that had spiked me on top of the pile.

I held it up in disgust.

Me: "Are you kidding me?"

Pete: "We just thought you'd become… attached to it."

Then they both collapsed in hysterics.

As a mature ten-year-old, I tried to appeal to their better nature.

Me *(in my head)*: "Sometimes you really should consider other people's feelings. If you take this attitude into adult life, you'll end up very, very lonely."

What I actually said:

"I'm telling my mum on you."

With that, I dropped the ice cream container like a mic.

Conkers scattered in every direction, making a bid for freedom.

Protest complete, I stormed out and slammed the garage door behind me.

Walking home, still fuming, I realised I was still holding that bloody COVID shell.

In a fit of rage, I hurled it against a wall.

CRACK!

It split clean in half, revealing a perfectly shaped, chestnut-brown, shiny conker.

Oh my God!

It was a mythical moment.

The conker seemed to levitate above the pavement, angels singing in the background.

This was no ordinary nut.

This was a sign.

That unassuming spiky shell had been trying to get my attention all along, and in one final act of redemption, it had split open to reveal…

'The King of Conkers'.

Or, as I named it: 'KOC'.

With my prize in hand, I headed home to plan my revenge on Pete and Jeremy.

The Vinegar Stroke of Genius

In the solitude of my shed, I gripped my KOC.

It was firm, but I needed it extra hard.

There was only one way to achieve this: 'The Vinegar Soak'.

I drilled a hole clean through the centre, threaded a piece of string, and suspended it in a jar of vinegar.

Not just any vinegar: Sarsons Extra Strength, the nuclear option.

I left it there for three whole days, transforming it into what I believed would be an unbreakable ball bearing.

When I finally pulled it out, I stared in horror.

My KOC had shrunk and shrivelled.

It looked like it had spent a weekend in the cold seawater at Barry Island.

Still, I was undeterred.

I picked up my wrinkled warrior, convinced that beneath its prune-like exterior, it was still forged of steel, and headed straight for Maes-Y-Cwm HQ.

The Hardest KOC on the Block

When I arrived, Jeremy was outside, parading his battle-scarred champion:

'Elevenses', undefeated in eleven conker contests.

Without hesitation, I challenged him to a street fight.

He accepted.

We stood toe-to-toe like two boxers in the ring, as referee Pete gave us the rules.

Pete: "I want a clean contest. No tugging, no hugging. Now touch conkers and come out swinging."

As reigning champ, Jeremy had first strike.

He looked smugly at my shrivelled offering, then swung with full force.

I closed my eyes and braced for impact.

Nothing?

I opened one eye to see Jeremy grimacing in pain, his eyes welling up.

He'd missed my conker entirely, and smashed his own into his elbow.

Jeremy *(screaming)*: "MUUUUM!"

Off he went to the HQ medical ward for a sticky plaster and a 'Mumsie cuddle'.

While he was gone, I indulged in a bit of shadow conkering, practising the ultimate knockout swing that would earn KOC the coveted title of 'Twelvesy'.

Jeremy returned, protesting like a man allergic to losing.

Jeremy *(whingeing)*: "His conker. It's too small. That's why I missed. It's unfair. He should be disqualified."

Pete: "Size isn't everything. Now get on with it!"

Jeremy huffed. Twice.

Then we stood toe-to-toe once more.

This time, it was my turn to strike.

I took aim, and with all my might, swung my would-be champion toward its opponent.

Somehow, it all happened in slow motion.

But instead of the satisfying crack of my conker smashing the reigning champion into a million pieces, there was silence.

Now, a tip for all aspiring conker champions:

Always remove the string before soaking your conker in vinegar.

Especially if it's Sarsons Extra Strength.

The string, weakened by the vinegar, snapped, launching KOC at full speed over Jeremy's shoulder.

The silence shattered as my conker began imitating a pinball machine, ricocheting off parked cars up and down the street.

I stood frozen, eyes wide, mouth agape, unable to comprehend what had just taken place.

Then came Jeremy's war cry, dragging me back to reality:

Jeremy *(chanting)*: "TWELVESY! TWELVESY! MY CONKER IS A TWELVESY!"

Still in shock, I slipped away from the street celebrations, my champion lost, my dignity dented.

I scoured gutters, gardens, driveways, desperate to be reunited with my shrivelled warrior, nothing.

Even after all these years, I've never stopped looking.

Once, I thought I'd found it.

Many years later, a tree had sprouted in a garden near Jeremy's house.

I dared to believe it had grown from the mighty King of Conkers.

But no!

It turned out to be a weeping willow.

Undeterred, I turned to social media for help.

I created a Facebook page:

"Have You Seen My KOC?"

The response was overwhelming, mostly from women.

Sadly, they all lived in Thailand… and weren't talking about conkers.

Steve Rowley

Nine Toenails

How to Lose Your Nail

Most people have ten toes and ten toenails.

Not me.

I've got ten toes and nine toenails.

I was born with the full set.

And if I still had all ten, I wouldn't be telling you this tale.

The Wheelie Years

Let's rewind to the mid-70s.

Mountain bikes didn't exist, so we improvised.

We took our racer bikes, ditched the drop handlebars, and replaced them with Cowhorn handlebars.

Just like that, we transformed Tour de France machines into Evel Knievel stunt bikes.

Struggling to picture Cowhorn handlebars?

Imagine Kate Winslet on the bow of the *Titanic*, arms outstretched, wind in her hair.

Now remove Leo, swap the *Titanic* for my mighty stunt bike, and there you have it: Kate Winslet, honorary member of our bike gang.

The beauty of the Cowhorn setup was the upright riding position, perfect for pulling back and lifting the front wheel to perform the holy grail of stunts: the Wheelie.

Commonplace now, revolutionary back then.

On two wheels, I was as fast as the next lad.

But on one wheel? Hopeless.

My mate Perry, on the other hand, could wheelie for eternity. To this day, I'm convinced his father was a unicycle.

My technique? Speed over balance.

The further I went, the faster I got.

I'd blast past Perry at Mach 1, front wheel barely skimming the ground, chasing that mythical moment of Total Balance.

It was my dream to join the Unicycle Fraternity Family. But dreams, as we know, often come at a cost.

Then, against all odds, after hundreds of failed attempts, I did it.

I raised my front wheel to the dizzying height of Total Balance.

Unfortunately, my front wheel had other ideas.

Not content with balance, it kept arcing backward, tipping me into an existential crisis.

I had two options:

    A. Overbalance and introduce the back of my head to Mr Tarmac.

    B. Jump off.

I chose the latter.

Jumping off was easy.

Landing at Mach 1? Not so much.

My feet slammed onto the tarmac, hitting the ground running at a speed only Usain Bolt could appreciate. Ouch.

I let go of the Cowhorns and began windmilling my arms like a deranged propeller, trying to stay upright and avoid a full-frontal faceplant.

Miraculously, I did it. I stayed upright.

So did my stunt bike, still on one wheel, disappearing into the sunset. I stood there, slowly waving *au revoir* to my silver stallion.

Then I felt it.

A warm, wet, throbbing sensation in the lower regions.

I looked down at my left Easy Breathe trainer and watched the material above my toes turn from grey to red.

Then the pain kicked in.

Unable to control the agony, I launched into my own rendition of Michael Flatley's *Riverdance*.

After a few impromptu dance routines, I managed to remove my trainer and the soggy, bloodstained sock.

The culprit?

The top edge of my toenail had sliced into the corner of my big toe.

Not that bad, I thought.

I'll be back on one wheel in no time.

Wrong.

Sister Grapple

Two months later, I was lying on an operating table at St Winifred's Hospital in Cardiff, having my ingrowing toenail removed under local anaesthetic.

The hospital also doubled as a nunnery, so penguin-like nurses glided around the ward with quiet authority.

The last time I saw that many penguins in one place, I was watching *Happy Feet*.

Looking around the operating theatre, I couldn't believe the number of scalpels at the disposal of my surgeon, Dr Edward Scissorhands.

Just as the procedure was about to begin, the theatre nun locked eyes with me:

Theatre Nun: "Look away from your foot, dear."

Unfortunately, I was at that age where being told to do something guaranteed I'd do the opposite.

So, as Dr Scissorhands began his work, I tilted my head for a sneaky peek at the carnage below.

Theatre Nun: "Oh no you don't, young man."

She pounced.

Before I knew it, I was in a full headlock, forced to look heavenward.

I was no match for Sister Grapple.

While locked in her holy grip, my mind wandered.

I felt oddly close to her, so close, I nearly asked the question that had haunted me since infant school:

"Why do YOU think God let me poo my pants on the way home from school, even after I prayed for help?"

At the last moment, I decided this was not the time or place.

Operation over, I arrived home to be greeted by Mum and a mug of tea.

Little did I know it was laced with six heaped spoonfuls of sugar.

I spat out the first mouthful.

Me *(shocked)*: "Mum! What are you trying to do to me?"

Mum *(sympathetically)*: "Sugar helps with shock."

Me: "Not in this case. I'm more shocked from the tea than I was by the operation."

The Double Header Tennis Match

A couple of months later, I felt normal again, which frankly was a novelty, as I've never been considered normal.

Still not ready to resume my unicycle duties, I turned to tennis.

It turns out I was far more talented on two feet with a racket in one hand than I ever was on one wheel, gripping Cowhorn handlebars with both.

As I ran out of worthy opponents, I began to believe the humble Gladstone Park Tennis Courts were merely a stepping stone to Centre Court at Wimbledon.

My unbeaten streak, two glorious matches, was about to be tested.

Two brothers challenged me.

Two against one.

I accepted.

The match was tense, riddled with cheating allegations, dramatic tantrums, and questionable line calls.

At two sets apiece, I found myself perched on match point, one swing away from Gladstone Park immortality.

Just before serving, I made a tactical masterstroke: switching from an underarm to an overarm.

The ball landed.

The brothers scrambled.

One of them, probably Colin, though it was hard to tell being conjoined twins, played a drop shot.

I sprinted, slid, and lunged.

I managed to return it, only for the ball to clip the top of the net.

Time slowed.

It rolled along the net tape, teetering between sides.

Colin anticipated long.

Brian anticipated short.

They froze.

The ball did a full pirouette, then dropped on their side of the court.

Victory was mine.

I leapt to my feet, arms raised to the gods.

The twins erupted into a ferocious argument, each blaming the other for the loss.

I considered stepping in to separate them, but lacking the surgical finesse of Dr Scissorhands, I left them to it.

Then I felt it.

That same warm, wet sensation I'd known the day my stunt bike vanished into the sunset.

My winning shot had come at a cost.

The freshly grown toenail had once again sliced into the corner of my left toe,

leaving me with yet another blood-soaked Easy Breathe Trainer, which was rapidly becoming more of an "Easy Bleed" trainer.

Sister Grapple 2 – Pleased to See You

A few weeks later, I found myself back at St Winifred's Hospital for round two, this time to have the toenail bed removed for good.

Timing, as ever, was not on my side.

I'd just turned sixteen and was deep in negotiations to purchase a Yamaha FS1E moped, my long-awaited ticket to motorised freedom.

On the way to the hospital, Dad and I made a detour to the City Motorcycle Showroom in Cardiff.

We paid.

I signed.

The FS1E was officially mine.

Uncle Mickey volunteered to ride it home.

With the ink still wet and the scent of two-stroke glory lingering in the air, I headed off to be reunited with Sister Grapple.

Cars, Chicks, and Nuns

Sitting upright in my hospital bed, I flipped through the latest issue of *Car and Car Conversions*, hoping to distract myself from the looming operation.

It featured the usual '*Car of the Month*', complete with a scantily dressed model draped across the bonnet.

Forgive me, I got a little excited. What more could a testosterone-fuelled sixteen-year-old want?

Then something unexpected popped up, nothing to do with the magazine.

Sister Grapple appeared. Magically.

Sister Grapple: "Right! I need to check your underwear, young man."

What the hell?

She yanked the privacy curtain around my bed with the speed of a pantomime stagehand.

Panic rising, I deployed my emergency mental distraction strategy: imagining the seventy-year-old nun sprawled across a car bonnet. Too late.

Without hesitation, she pulled back the sheets.

There they were, my novelty nylon pants, proudly emblazoned with a vibrant, undeniably enthusiastic "Pleased to See You" message across the front, complete with 3D graphic emphasis. Let's just say they were doing exactly what they were designed to do.

Sister Grapple, trained in the art of unflinching calm under bizarre circumstances, did not blink.

Sister Grapple: "Right! You'll have to take those off."

I froze, recreating the *Home Alone* look of horror.

Sister Grapple: "No nylon in theatre. Have you brought any cotton underwear?"

Me *(stammering)***:** "Nnnno. Sorry."

Sister Grapple: "I'll be back." And off she went.

I yanked the sheets back into place faster than you could say Holy Humiliation, hoping to spare my fellow ward-mates any unwanted glimpses of my 'Stun-the-Nun' pants of shame.

No sooner had I swapped my car magazine for the *Gospel of Matthew* than Sister Grapple returned, this time wielding a pair of extra-large pink cotton knickers.

Sister Grapple: "These are the only cotton pants available. You're next in theatre, so pop them on."

No negotiations. Zero options.

I inspected my new modesty protectors.

They weren't pants, they were canvas sails.

Presumably designed for a very large lady whose backside had its own postcode.

I fell into them.

The waistband settled just below my collarbone, while the lower regions enjoyed full exposure to the crisp hospital air.

There I lay, a vision in blush pink stretch cotton, waiting on a trolley in the pre-op room, praying the theatre staff would be merciful and not remove my dignity along with my toenail bed.

Just as I adjusted my gown to cover up 'Planet Pink', Sister Grapple reappeared, with backup.

Sister Grapple: "This is Lisa. She'll be looking after you in theatre."

I looked up.

Nurse Lisa.

Early twenties. Slim. Tall. Beautiful brown eyes. Definitely car-bonnet material.

She began stroking my leg reassuringly, then leaned in to speak.

Mask pulled down, she unleashed a smile so radiant it nearly resuscitated my self-esteem.

I felt the urge to climb off the trolley and propose, only my pink knickers held me back.

Nurse Lisa: "Hi Steve, don't worry! I'll be right by your side through the operation."

Her gentle touch and soothing words turned pre-op panic into a scene from a teenage rom-com set in a surgical theatre.

I nodded, trying to remain composed, pink pants and all.

She began to pull her mask back on, but hesitated.

I could feel it, she had something else to say.

I gave her my Steve McQueen cheeky grin. Play it cool, Steve. Don't make a fool of yourself.

Nurse Lisa *(smirking)*: "Oh! I forgot to ask…"

Pregnant pause.

"Sister Grapple told me about your replacement knickers. Are they comfortable?"

She flashed a cheeky grin of her own.

My smirk wilted into a grimace.

Me *(quietly, through gritted teeth)*: "Beam me up, Scotty."

The anaesthetist leaned in.

Anaesthetist: "Okay Steve, you'll start to feel drowsy, then you'll be asleep within ten seconds."

Needle inserted.

Nurse Lisa: "Okay Steve, count to ten with me."

And just like that, seven was the final word of our theatrical duet. Her voice drifted off as the anaesthetic did its thing.

The Great Delayed Escape

Next thing I knew, Scotty had done his job.

I was back in bed on the ward.

The anaesthetist did his checks, gave the thumbs-up, then left. Time to initiate the escape plan.

But before Operation Dignity could commence, Sister Grapple reappeared at the foot of my bed.

Sister Grapple: "I'll be back in a moment, Steven, to sort you out."

Panic mode: engaged.

Surely she was coming back to retrieve her knickers.

And giving a nun her knickers back just didn't sit right with me.

I reached for my Stun-the-Nun pants, vanished under the sheets, and began the great knicker swap of 1979.

Ignoring the pain of tugging elastic over my newly nail-less toe, I emerged victorious, pink knickers respectfully placed on the side table just as Sister Grapple returned.

Phew.

She checked my blood pressure, picked up the pink parachute at arm's length, and vanished like the benevolent Ghost of Wardrobe Mishaps Past.

Too late to discharge me that day, so I had to wait until dawn to escape.

All I had to do was sleep.

What else could possibly go wrong?

I'm glad you asked.

A Lump Too Far

At midnight, I was jolted awake by a sound like a toothless Labrador gnawing on a marrowbone.

With the ward lights dimmed, it took a second or two to focus.

The Indian gentleman across from me, recovering from a nose operation, had partially swallowed his nasal dressing in his sleep, then coughed it up through his mouth.

There he sat, upright, with a blood-soaked rag dangling from his lips.

Blood dripped onto the bed.

He looked like one of Freddy Krueger's victims.

No nuns in sight. I hit the attention button. Nothing.

Only one option: run for help.

Or in my case, hobble like Long John Silver looking for his wooden leg.

Down the corridor, I found two nurses emerging from another ward.

Me *(panicking)*: "Freddy Krueger's on the loose. One of his victims needs help."

One nurse sprinted ahead. I hobbled behind.

The other lingered at her desk before catching up.

Desk Nurse: "Had a bit of an accident then?"

Me: "Yes. Hopefully, all sorted now."

Desk Nurse *(comedian mode)*: "Nice underwear."

Bugger!

In all the Freddy frenzy, I'd forgotten what I was wearing, a theatre gown with an open back, proudly exposing the rear of my Stun-the-Nun pants.

I shifted the front of my gown to inspect. What the hell?

The 3D print was gone.

Had Sister Grapple performed graphic surgery mid-op?

Nope.

Turns out, in my rush to switch pants, I'd put them on backwards.

The 3D print now proudly adorned the back of my pants, creating a lump that defied medical classification.

I got back into bed and buried myself under the sheets, praying for morning to arrive quickly and mercifully.

Riding and Grinding

The next day, I limped into the safe haven called home.

Mum greeted her little soldier like a returning war hero.

Mum: "Tea?"

Me: "Six sugars?"

Mum: "Yes."

Me: "Brilliant."

Home alone, recovering from my eventful toenail bed removal, I sat with my bandaged foot elevated like a fallen warrior, surrounded by sweet tea and daytime telly. It didn't take long for boredom to strike.

Just a short hobble away sat my Yamaha FS1E, tucked safely in Uncle Mickey's garage, whispering promises of freedom.

No Mum.

No Dad.

No Sister Grapple.

No sense.

'Operation Stealth' was born.

I slipped on one trainer and plastic-bagged the bandaged foot like I was protecting a gourmet sandwich.

Donkey jacket on.

Crutches under arms.

Crash helmet securely wobbling. Mission activated.

Now, it wasn't quite SAS-level stealth, where capture results in German SS officers removing my remaining toenails with pliers.

No. This would be far worse: answering to Mum.

Off I set on my covert mission.

Mental image check:

- Sixteen years old
- Six foot two
- Ten stone of nothing
- Dressed like an Irish workman
- Revolving crash helmet
- On crutches

Basically, I looked like The Stig's homeless cousin, on a covert limp through Barry Town.

I reached the garage.

There it was: the mighty Yamaha FS1E, a moped sent from motorcycle heaven.

The key was in the ignition.

The Floating Frog

I discarded the crutches like a soldier rejecting peacetime.

Kickstarted it with the good foot and it fired into life.

In my head? It sounded like a quartet of lions.

In reality? A mosquito with attitude.

The urge to ride the bike became too much. I felt the 'Need for Speed'.

To ride the FS1E, I needed a gear-shifting workaround.

Pushing down was easy.

Pushing up? Not so much, too close to the battle-scarred toe.

Solution: use my heel to shift upward.

With the FS1E off its stand, I checked for ground clearance, enough room to heel-shift without my plastic-wrapped toe grazing the tarmac. Problem solved. Victory!

All morning, I rode the local streets, heel-shifting with growing swagger. Not ideal technique, but I was mobile and loving it.

Then, during a pit stop outside Uncle Mickey's garage, Peter rocked up on his Suzuki TS50.

I was so chuffed to show off my Dream Machine, I offered him a spin.

As Peter tore off on my Yamaha, I leapt onto his Suzuki and gave chase.

That's when reality dropped a gear.

On the first corner, I instinctively heel-shifted, same move I'd nailed all morning.

But the Suzuki had its own agenda.

My nail-less toe, enclosed only in the supermarket plastic bag, met the tarmac.

I let out a roar that could've turned the lion quartet into a barbershop quintet.

My toe dragged along the road like a carrot through a cheese grater.

After what seemed an eternity of excruciating pain, I managed to pull over.

I gingerly laid the Suzuki on the ground, collapsed on the kerb, and stared down at my foot, hesitating, bargaining, praying.

Quick tip: Supermarket plastic bags are not a substitute for steel-capped biker boots. Ever.

No need to unwrap the damage.

The road had already shredded the bag, my blood-soaked toe poked through like a hot chip dunked in tomato sauce.

Battling against the pain, I hobbled back to the garage and sat on the floor at the foot of the steps, foot elevated above my head, resting on the top step, praying gravity would stem the flow of ketchup.

That's when Peter burst through the garage, wild-eyed.

Peter *(annoyed)*: "Why the hell is my bike lying on the road!?" Then he spotted the toe.

Peter: "Holy shite! What happened?"

I explained the subtle differences between the height of the Yamaha and the Suzuki gear levers. The Suzuki did not have the heel-shift option.

Peter crouched down to inspect the wound.

Peter: "Yuck! What are those little black creatures swimming in the blood?"

Me: "Creatures?"

We peered closer. Then the penny dropped.

Me: "Oh bollocks… they're my stitches."

We counted: 1, 2, 3, 4.

Peter: "How many did you have?"

Me: "Four."

Peter: "Well, at least that saves the district nurse the trouble of removing them."

Me: "Hilarious! Now I've got to explain this to Mum."

Peter: "Good luck, mate. You're on your own."

Peter picked up his Suzuki and took off in the opposite direction.

Bastard!

I hobbled home. Mum opened the door.

Mum: "Where have you been?"

Me: "Got bored. Went for a hop."

She eyed the sad attempt at a rewrapped toe.

Mum: "What have you done you silly boy?"

Me: "Tripped over."

She wasn't buying it.

Mum: "Really? Uncle Mickey just phoned. Asked why your bike was off the stand and if I knew anything about the blood on the garage steps."

Operation Stealth: compromised.

I confessed and showed Mum the toe, minus stitches.

Her disappointment melted into concern.

She knew just the cure: Epsom salts in boiling hot water.

As my foot descended into the molten bowl, the pain intensified to the point where I'd have preferred the SS officer with pliers.

Moments later, she handed me a mug of tea.

Me: "Six sugars?"

Mum: "Of course."

Me: "Brilliant."

I clutched the mug with both hands, sipping like it contained the secrets of the universe.

Did the tea help?

As they say, Mum knows best.

Over the years, many have said my toe resembles a finalist in a Gurney Face competition.

One thing's certain, it wouldn't win a beauty pageant.

Smoking

Willy Wonka and The Cigarette Factory

Pete and I were walking home from Barry Island Funfair, taking a shortcut across Barry Docks, when we stumbled upon a tin of Golden Virginia hand-rolling tobacco near the dock entrance, probably dropped by some poor docker on his way to work.

As 14-year-old boys, we were at precisely the wrong age to make correct decisions.

I picked the tin up quickly and tucked it under my jumper. We darted into the nearest back lane to investigate our treasure.

It felt like a scene straight out of *Willy Wonka and the Chocolate Factory*, that moment when Charlie opens his bar of chocolate and finds the Golden Ticket.

I carefully prised open the tin, hoping it still had its contents. A golden glow seemed to rise from within.

There it was.

Pete and I *(in unison)*: "Tobacco."

Just like Charlie ignoring the warning on the Wonka bar, "Chocolate can make you fat, so don't blame your thyroid", we were about to ignore the warning on the tin: "Smoking can seriously kill you."

We stared at our treasure for a moment.

Pete: "What Now?"

I looked at him in disbelief.

Me *(sarcastically)***:** "What do you mean, 'What now?' I know - let's empty the tobacco onto the floor so you can use the tin to store your marbles."

I shook my head.

Me: "Smoke it, of course."

Now, up until this point, I'd never had the urge to smoke.

Well… that's not entirely true.

Interlude:

There was that time Pete and I borrowed my dad's pipe while he was out. According to TV ads in the seventies, smoking a pipe made you interesting, and, more importantly, irresistible to incredibly attractive women.

Naturally, we had to test the theory.

You might be forgiven for thinking that a pimply-faced, skinny teenager wearing:

- Purple platform shoes
- Patch pocket trousers
- A long woollen cardigan
- A bobbleless bobble cap
- And enough Old Spice aftershave to fumigate a small village

…was not exactly a magnet for the opposite sex.

But hey, it was the 70s. And I thought I was cool.

But cool wasn't enough. I needed to become an irresistible force.

And to achieve that status, all I needed was one final accessory:

A Pipe.

Yep, I pictured myself strutting around town, puffing on my pipe, playing 'Pick a Chick' from the hordes of women chasing me, fighting for my attention, just like the St Bruno pipe tobacco adverts had promised.

Still not convinced how cool I looked?

Try this:

Take a deep breath.

Now slowly nod your head up and down.

Keep nodding as you re-read this list:

- Purple platform shoes
- Patch pocket trousers
- A long woollen cardigan
- A bobbleless bobble cap
- The overpowering stench of Old Spice
- And of course… puffing on a pipe

Subconsciously, that nodding has tricked your brain into thinking:

"You know what? He totally is 70s cool."

With my dad's pipe and his tobacco in our possession, Pete and I got to work. We filled the pipe to the brim. I pressed the tobacco down with all my might until I couldn't cram in another flake. Then I struck a match, ready to light our way to sophistication.

I sucked and sucked until I was blue in the face… but the bloody pipe wouldn't light.

I handed it to Pete. Same result.

Two boxes of matches later, we had to accept defeat.

It just didn't happen like this on the TV ads.

There was only one thing for it: get my older sister Linda to light it for us.

After a lot of persuading, and a solemn promise to do her dusting and vacuuming chores for the next week, she agreed.

Linda grabbed the pipe, inspected the contents, then promptly removed half the tobacco.

Linda *(sarcastically)*: "It's all about airflow, you idiot." She struck a match, gave it two puffs and sophistication was lit.

As she handed the pipe back, she couldn't resist a parting shot:

Linda: "A week off chores! Sometimes it's good to have a moron for a brother." She disappeared back into the house, laughing like Cruella de Vil.

Pete: "Who's going first?"

Me: "I'm doing all the housework this week, so it's me."

Still muttering about my sister, I put the pipe in my mouth and drew a tentative breath.

As the smoke entered my lungs, I suddenly felt an overwhelming urge to swap my purple platform shoes for a comfy pair of leather sandals.

By the fifth puff, I was convinced I could complete a crossword, with actual letters, not just colouring in the empty boxes.

I handed the pipe to Pete and lay down on the grass, basking in my newfound sophistication.

Poetry, I thought. I should write poetry.

And with that, I spontaneously composed the first line of my debut masterpiece:

"Awake, it's day, say the Cocks on the Farm."

Poetically Challenged

"Awake, it's day…" was the opening line of my one and only attempt at poetry.

I didn't have a spontaneous Dylan Thomas moment.

I was forced to write a poem for an English assignment. Unable to match the grandeur of a classical opening line… I failed the assignment.

Smoke affects.

A strange taste began to develop in my mouth. I swished saliva from side to side, trying to identify it. Then, without warning, it exploded into a hideously vile flavour.

I can only describe it as what I imagine it would taste like to kiss the Pope's ring… after it had been kissed by a thousand people before.

The taste triggered a full-body retch.

I ran to the garden tap to water down the happenings in my mouth. Bugger, the hose was still attached.

In desperation, I turned the tap on and drank straight from the hose. Holy Mother of God!

Stagnant hose water is not a substitute for mouthwash.

As the PVC-infused liquid hit the back of my throat, my brain sent an urgent message to my stomach:

Brain: "Incoming."

Stomach: "Absolutely not."

The fight between my throat and stomach reached a stalemate. Then my nasal cavity joined the conflict.

So, there I was, on my hands and knees, liquid pouring from every orifice, retching like a man possessed. This was definitely not part of the script according to the TV advert.

Meanwhile, in another part of the garden, the mystical powers of the pipe had a completely different effect on Pete. He was now strolling around, pipe in mouth, reading aloud the complete works of William Shakespeare to the 'rhododendrons'.

After that episode, pipe smoking was history for me. In the end, I had to settle for being 70s cool, pipe-free, poetry-free, and slightly traumatised.

Pete still swears Shakespeare spoke to him that day.

Outerlude:

Where was I?…

Back to the tin of Wonka tobacco.

We knew our treasure was worthless without Rizla cigarette papers. They were the missing ingredient, the sacred scrolls that would allow us to manufacture our own smokes.

Digging deep, we scraped together 87p between us. This was money our parents had given us for chips for dinner (old school). But we figured we had more than enough for a pack of Rizlas and a box of matches.

So Pete and I made the ultimate sacrifice: we gave up our bag of chips for a hot cigarette sandwich instead.

We marched into the nearest newsagent and asked for a pack of Rizlas and a box of matches. The shopkeeper gave us a long, menacing stare.

Shopkeeper *(sarcastically)*: "Bit young to be smoking, boys?"

Caught off guard.

Me *(hesitating)*: "No! It's… it's for my dad. Yes. My dad."

The shopkeeper didn't blink.

Shopkeeper: "Oh look - there's a cow with wings behind you. Best get your dad to do his own shopping. Off you go boys."

We parted ways with the friendly shopkeeper, totally dejected.

But we weren't giving up.

We walked to another newsagent. Outside the shop, I turned to Pete.

Me: "I've got this. You stay here."

I entered the shop and approached the little old lady behind the counter with my best impression of innocence.

Me *(overly polite)*: "Hello. Please may I have a tube of chocolate Smarties… and, oh yes, my mum asked me to get some Cigarette papers? I think that's what she called them - Rizlas? And a box of matches, please."

Result!

She fell for it. Served me with a smile. I paid, and I was on my way.

One Puff Too Many

Back in the back lanes, Pete and I began our cigarette-making apprenticeship.

Unlike the cowboys or Steve McQueen types on TV, who could roll a perfect cigarette one-handed and strike a match on the sole of their boot, we were just two pimple-faced teenagers in Barry, fumbling like we were trying to defuse a bomb.

We laid a Rizla flat on the lid of the tin, then placed a strip of tobacco along the edge. That part was easy.

Using my index fingers (yes, the nose-picking ones), I gently rolled the edges of the paper and the tobacco into a scroll.

Pete placed his own nose-picking finger on the centre of the scroll, allowing me to release my fingers. I re-gripped the ends. Pete moved his finger. I lifted the scroll to my mouth and gently applied spit glue.

The cigarette was born.

It wasn't pretty. But neither were we.

With my neck locked in anticipation, I placed one end of the cigarette between my lips. Pete struck a match and slowly raised it toward the other end.

The tension was unbearable. My lips quivered as the flame approached.

Pete *(whispering)*: "Come on…"

Then, just as flame and cigarette were about to become one, the bloody thing collapsed.

All the tobacco fell to the floor, leaving me with a limp Rizla paper stuck to my lip, flapping in the wind like a surrender flag.

Pete stood frozen, still holding the match where the end of the cigarette had been moments earlier.

Standing there on a mound of spilled tobacco, with my sister Linda nowhere in sight, we had no choice but to concede defeat.

We headed home, dejected, with a near-empty tin of tobacco and half a box of matches. The main topic of conversation: what could have been.

As we passed the Memorial Hall gardens on the way home, a gap in the clouds appeared. A single ray of sunshine beamed down onto a small bush.

We stopped.

Its leaves were golden brown, and, to our amazement, they were curled into the exact shape of pre-rolled Rizla papers.

This was definitely a sign.

We picked a leaf, stuffed it with the remaining tobacco, and moments later, there it was:

Rowley's Rollie.

The most perfect-looking cigarette ever created. So perfect, I was reluctant to light it.

Pete *(impatient)*: "Go on then."

"Smoke it."

I placed it between my lips and struck a match.

Within two puffs, Rowley's Rollie burst into life.

I had finally come of age. I was now a fully-fledged member of the cool fraternity.

The third puff… didn't go quite so well.

The clouds closed. The ray of sunshine vanished.

A little dog walked by… and pissed on the bush.

Oh my God. What was happening?

I dropped to my knees, clawing at the grass like a man trying to anchor himself to Earth as the world began to spin.

Faster and faster.

Reaching speeds in excess of Fast Spin on a washing machine.

After what seemed an eternity, the world slowed enough that I no longer feared being launched into orbit.

I released my white-knuckle grip on the grass.

Pete: "Well? What was it like?"

The only words I could manage:

Me: "I think I'm going to die. Take me home."

By the time we got back to my house, my saliva, missing since the world started spinning, had returned.

But it brought with it a grotesque, sewage-like taste that made me instantly vomit.

I thought the pipe experience was bad.

But compared to Rowley's Rollie, the pipe-and-hose-water cocktail tasted like angel mouthwash.

That was the end of that episode.

Pete disappeared with the tin, now repurposed for his marble collection.

Since that day, I've never smoked again.

Ironically, I ended up working in a cigar factory.

Life's strange sometimes.

91

Push Biking

Silly Stunt

The Golden Arrow, my first bike, and the beginning of my love affair with two wheels.

At four years old, I spent every spare moment exploring the local streets with my best friend: the Golden Arrow.

I was at that age when talking to your bike felt perfectly normal.

If it could've grown with me, I'd still have it today.

One of my favourite dares was riding all the way from the local sweet shop to my street without touching the brakes.

The direct route? Western Hill, a steep descent at the far end of my street.

Far too dangerous for this dare.

So instead, I took the backstreets running parallel to it, gradually picking up speed before a sharp right onto Rectory Road, then it was full-blown toboggan mode.

The bottom stretch of Rectory Road levelled out, and I figured it was just long enough to slow down, without brakes, before reaching the finishing line: my street, Charlotte Place.

So many times, I reached the blind corner at the start of Rectory Road, but for one reason or another, I'd tap the brake lever, which meant game over.

Then the day of reckoning arrived.

With a pocket full of American hard gums, I headed home from the sweet shop.

At the top of Western Hill, I turned into Everard Street, the first of the backstreets, with a slight uphill gradient.

No brakes so far.

Interlude:

Coincidentally, number 11 Everard Street was my first home.

The street that gave me my porn star name: Bobby Ever'ard.

Name of your first pet, then the first street you lived on.

Now that's a proper porn star name, could even double as a Viagra brand.

I can't really remember living there, probably because I was still a rug rat when Mum and Dad moved us to Charlotte Place.

The removal company they used?

None other than Harry the Milkman and his electric milk float.

In the good old days, the milkman was an integral part of local society, the ultimate neighbourhood watch.

Not just delivering milk in all weather, but relaying local news, checking on the elderly, and quietly keeping a pulse on the street.

A milkman wasn't just a delivery man, he was everybody's friend.

Then came the cartons.

Difficult to open. And they never asked how your nan was doing.

And just like that, the milkman vanished.

End of an era.

Outerlude:

Where was I…?

The beginning of the Toboggan run.

Everard Street was easy, no brakes required.

Then I turned right into Guys Road, the downhill journey started.

No pedalling from this point onwards.

Gaining a little speed, I turned left into Tydfil Street.

Momentum was becoming the enemy as I rapidly approached the right turn into Rectory Road.

This was the point I'd usually tap the brakes, but not today.

Today, I entered Rectory Road without braking.

What happened next is just a blur.

All I remember is: sky, tarmac, sky, tarmac.

I had absolutely no idea what had gone wrong, but there I was, lying on the ground, face to face with the tarmac.

Strangely, I still remember my nose resting on a flattened piece of chewed-up, spat-out chewing gum stuck to the tarmac.

After a brief moment of silence, I realised I was entangled with the crumpled Golden Arrow, limbs and levers all in the wrong place.

Unable to break free, I assessed my predicament and decided my best option was to scream. Loudly.

The next thing I remember, a few people were standing around me. They seemed to appear from nowhere.

I started to panic.

I could hear a man explaining to a woman what he'd witnessed:

Man *(reporter mode)*: "I was walking my dog, Rusty, along the pavement when, out of the blue, this poor little fellow came flying around the corner. I think his brakes failed. His front wheel started wobbling, then, whoosh!, he somehow flew over the handlebars while still holding on to them. Bounced down the road a couple of times before ending up like this. I think he's going to need an X-ray."

The word *X-ray* meant only one thing: ray guns and stitches.

Cue blind panic.

Then, in the distance, I saw Mum and Dad running towards me.

Dad managed to untangle me from the bent and twisted Golden Arrow.

Once free, Mum scooped me up and cuddled me.

Mum: "What have you done, you silly boy? I could hear you screaming from our house!"

All I could do was respond in one of those gulping, can't-catch-my-breath conversations that made absolutely no sense.

As the panic faded slightly, it was replaced by a stabbing pain in my side, just above my hip.

Eventually, I managed to draw Mum's attention to the area using the pointy finger on my right hand.

She lifted my woolly jumper slowly.

Yep, another blood-soaked shirt.

This was becoming an unwelcome habit.

She lifted my shirt very, very slowly…

The moment was like a game show host keeping the audience suspended with that annoying, pregnant pause before revealing the result.

Well, in this situation, the winner was a small chunk of flesh missing from the top of my hip, blood oozing out like ketchup from a shaken bottle.

Mum: "Oh my God! Dad, look at this wound!"

Dad examined my bike injury.

Dad: "Tis but a scratch."

Now, Dad is old school, so unless my kidney was lying on the floor next to me, a Band-Aid plaster was more than adequate medical intervention.

So the repair work involved no more than a quick soak in Epsom salts and a comically oversized Band-Aid.

The incident left me with a lifelong scar above my hip.

But here's the twist: the scar actually looks like a flattened piece of chewed-up and spat-out chewing gum, eerily similar to the one that had been stuck to the tarmac under my nose on the day of my accident.

Did I learn anything from this incident?

Well, the answer is simple.

No!

Still a Silly Stunt

A few years later, on another bike, I dared to ride down Western Hill, this time, using the brakes.

But the challenge was this:

How far from the turn into Charlotte Place could I release the brake, then freewheel at speed, take the corner without touching the brakes, without clipping the kerb, and without being catapulted into the gardens of the flats at the bottom of our street?

What was I thinking?

Clearly, I'd left my brain at the top of the hill.

On the way home from school, I decided to set a new world record:

Freewheeling around-the-corner at speed without brakes.

Almost at a standstill, I released the brakes, twenty metres from the turn.

The bike accelerated rapidly downhill, and by the time I reached the corner at Charlotte Place… it was too late to abort the mission.

It was like a parachute jump:

"Once you've jumped, you've jumped."

Unfortunately, I didn't have an emergency ripcord to pull as I hurtled towards a brand-new Ford Cortina parked outside the flats.

I braced for impact.

At the last moment, before bike and car became one, I turned parallel to the vehicle, hit the driver's door with my pedal, bounced off the side, and, in one motion, leapt from the bike without stopping…

Then bolted up the street, pushing it like a getaway vehicle.

When I got home to an empty house, I opened the front door, parked the bike in the hallway, slammed the door shut, and sat on the stairs, staring at the front door in silence.

I waited nervously, expecting the Ford's owner to arrive, fists clenched, vengeance monologue rehearsed.

"When I find you, I will lay my vengeance upon thee."

(Very Quentin Tarantino.)

Luckily, Samuel L. Jackson didn't come knocking.

I inspected the damage. The impact had bent my pedal right under the frame, making it impossible to ride.

The handlebars were misaligned, but I managed a DIY fix, holding the front wheel between my knees and wrenching the bars back into place.

Had my parents found out, there'd be no cuddling this time.

They'd have marched me back to the scene and personally hand-fed me to Samuel L. Jackson as punishment for fleeing a self-inflicted felony.

The next day, I confessed to Dad: I'd had an accident, and the pedal needed fixing.

Yes, I told him I'd hit a kerb on the way to school, trying to avoid a cute puppy that had darted into the road.

Result! Dad bought it. Hook, line, and puppy.

He drove me to school.

Picked me up.

And when I got home, the pedal had been replaced.

Dad, proud of his son's selflessness, risking life and limb to save a helpless mutt, had bought and fitted two brand-new pedals onto my bike.

Did I forget to mention that the flats at the bottom of Charlotte Place were, in fact, police flats?

Prison sentence avoided.

Let's jump back to the Golden Arrow Saga.

The bike never seemed to ride nicely after the chewing-gum incident.

Maybe it was cursed.

Or maybe it just knew I was still a silly stunt waiting to happen.

The Bike, The Myth, The Heartbreak.

I was eight years old, and Christmas was a couple of months away.

It was the era when everyone who was anyone had a Raleigh Chopper. The Chopper was *The Bike King*, every boy's dream.

That was every boy… except me.

I had fallen in love with a Schwinn dragster bike, the American version of the Raleigh Chopper.

It was for sale in a bike shop I walked past on the way home from school.

Every day, without fail, I'd go into the shop and spend five minutes sitting on the Schwinn, with its golden tassels hanging from the ends of the handlebars, imagining myself pulling up alongside my mates, all riding their Raleigh Choppers.

Then, with my hair tied back in a ponytail, chewing gum, I'd remove my sunglasses in a cool way, greeting them with:

"What's occurring?"

Sunglasses and chewing gum were possible…

But the ponytail was a bit far-fetched.

I could never have grown my hair long enough without looking like Susan Boyle.

Every time I left the bike shop, the guy who worked there would shout to me, "It'll soon be Christmas!"

Every single day in our house, it was Schwinn bike this and Schwinn bike that. It was all I could talk about.

In the end, Mum had had enough.

Mum: "You can stop talking about it, Steve. We know what you want for Christmas."

Then she winked at Dad.

Oh my God, it was really going to happen.

All I could picture was Susan Boyle in sunglasses, cruising around the streets of Barry on an American Schwinn dragster bike.

Christmas couldn't come quick enough.

I don't think I stopped smiling for a whole week leading up to Father Christmas's visit.

So you can picture my crushing disappointment that Christmas morning, walking into the front room only to discover not the Susan Boyle–inspired American dragster, but a girlie step-through bicycle, proudly equipped with the indispensable football-transport accessory: a dainty shopping basket perched over the rear wheel.

Hanging from the handlebars was a tag that read:

"Merry Christmas, Steve. Love from Father Christmas."

Father Bloody Christmas had done it again.

Unable to contain my disappointment, Mum fled to the kitchen in tears, followed by Dad, performing his silently shouting routine.

This was starting to become a Christmas tradition.

Not even a game of *Kerplunk* could lift me from my deep depression.

I hated that bloody girlie step-through pushbike.

But if I wanted to be part of the gang, I needed wheels.

Those wheels, minus the cute shopping basket (hindsight: this would have come in very handy for conkering), stayed with me for nearly three years… until I finally saved enough pocket money to part-exchange it for a full-sized bike: a Carlton five-speed racer.

Bikes and Flights

Turns out, when I sat on the saddle of the Carlton, I couldn't reach the pedals.

So, for a few months, I cycled on a knife edge, using the crossbar as a temporary metal saddle.

I was balanced precariously between coolness and chafing.

This was the very bike that modified the bodywork on the Ford Cortina parked outside the police flats.

It was also the bike that was responsible for nine toenails.

But before losing the toenail, the Carlton added another scar to my collection.

Pete and I often took the docks road home from school. There wasn't much traffic along the stretch we used.

Railway tracks ran diagonally across the road, embedded in the tarmac, so you could ride over them comfortably.

Comfortably… if you were holding the handlebars.

Since the road was quiet, Pete and I made a competition out of it:

Who could ride the furthest and fastest no-handed?

OK, I think you know what's coming.

Unfortunately, I didn't.

As I hurtled along no-handed at full speed, my front wheel suddenly decided it was a train, veering violently right to follow the tracks. One moment I was riding a bike; the next, we'd parted company and I was airborne, arms outstretched like Superman.

My flight was brief. I soared over a mound of kryptonite, instantly stripped of my powers, and plunged into a swallow dive, earthbound, hands first, straight onto the tarmac.

The landing was… less than heroic.

But pride took precedence.

I sprang to my feet, casually ignoring the fresh agony radiating from my left elbow.

Pete: "What the hell was that all about?"

Me: "My bike decided to go trainspotting."

Pete: "You've hurt your arm, then?"

(Trying to cover up my embarrassment.)

Me *(in denial)***:** "No."

Pete: "Well, there's blood dripping from your left hand…"

The moment I saw it, the pain caught up, amplified by the sight of crimson proof.

I peeled off my school blazer with theatrical slowness… revealing yet another blood-soaked shirt.

Yep, another chewing-gum scar, this time on my left elbow.

A permanent souvenir from my first unaided solo flight.

A Straightforward Bike

Some time later, I removed the front wheel from my Carlton bike.

Not to punish it for thinking it was a train wheel, but to build a three-wheel tandem using my bike and Pete's bike.

No clue what inspired us. Probably boredom.

I bent my front forks outwards and slotted them onto the spindle of Pete's rear wheel.

Sounds simple, but it took us most of Saturday morning to coax two stubborn machines into a single entity.

By dinnertime (old school), we had created the world's first three-inline-wheel tandem.

Drunk on excitement and engineering pride, we pushed our invention out of the shed and onto the road.

Pete climbed on the front. I mounted the rear.

On the count of three, we pedalled.

It wobbled.

But the faster we went, the steadier it felt.

What an achievement!

Clearly, we had to get back to my house and begin the patent process before someone spotted us and stole the idea.

That's when things unravelled.

We tried turning around, but the tandem refused to cooperate.

When the front wheel turned, the middle and rear kept going straight, launching us off.

After five more falls, we surrendered, to logic, and to the laws of steering.

We had built a one-way mode of transport.

Totally dejected, Pete and I dismantled our creation, reassembled our original bikes, and parted ways, as did the path to fame and fortune.

We genuinely believed our design would revolutionise the cycling world.

Turns out, the cycling world wasn't ready for a bike that couldn't turn.

Trade of the Weak

Even after five years of reckless ownership, full of highs and very painful lows, my Carlton five-speed racer was still a sought-after bike.

I discovered this one afternoon as I passed the second-hand shop where I'd swapped it for a £10 full-face crash helmet.

There it was, proudly displayed in the front window, now sporting gleaming drop handlebars and a smug little price tag: £60.

My *Trade of the Weak.*

I walked away, crash helmet in hand, wondering if horsepower would be any less painful than pedal power.

Spoiler alert: it wasn't.

Motor Biking

Born to Be Mild

My motorbiking exploits could never compete with the rebellious, leather-clad legend of *Born to Be Wild*.

Mine were more *Carry On Kickstarting*, same two wheels, just with less leather and more acne.

The day before my 16th birthday, I received my provisional driving licence: a flimsy piece of paper that promised motorised freedom on the open road.

So, to the beginning.

What came first, the motorbike or the crash helmet?

With licence in hand, the next essential ingredient in my fuelled-up recipe for freedom was head protection.

I found the perfect match, yep, the £10 blue full-face helmet I swapped for my Carlton pushbike.

After a bit of haggling, the deal was sealed.

And when I say haggling, the shopkeeper simply asked,

"Are you sure you want to swap?"

It looked like it had been passed around more than a karaoke mic on a Friday night. The fitting process was rudimentary: get it over my ears, and I was ready for any Crash Test Dummy mission.

Actually, when I put it on, it felt like it rested on my shoulders rather than the top of my head. But hey, it was within budget.

Now, proudly armed with a crash helmet, all I needed was the final ingredient: a motorbike. After a few weeks of searching, I found the perfect companion, the never-to-be-forgotten Yamaha FS1E.

(The machine responsible for my gurney-faced big toe.)

I bought it in 1979 for £180.

It was 50cc of pure fizz, the engine pushing out a staggering 4.8 horsepower.

That's nearly five horses.

Not sure what breed they were, because 4.8 horsepower is roughly equivalent to two electric hairdryers.

Maybe they based it on seahorses?

My crash helmet still had its pull-down visor, which, everyone knows, is a vital part of the helmet's safety integrity.

The visor had a yellow tint. I don't think this was factory standard; more likely the result of ageing plastic.

It reduced visibility to about 70 percent. I figured at least it was better than 50.

Another important feature of the visor: it stopped the rushing air from spinning the helmet around my head when I hit speeds above 20 mph.

If I rode with the visor up, the wind would get inside the ill-fitting helmet and try to spin it like a weather vane.

Luckily, my parents had bestowed upon me a long nose.

When the helmet tried to rotate past 45 degrees, my nose would catch on the side of the lookie-out bit and act as a stopper.

Many a time, I'd be riding down the road, one eye hidden inside the helmet, the other guiding me forward, while the helmet pointed at shop windows, giving the illusion I was window shopping rather than concentrating on the road ahead. It was not a good look.

That said, the helmet did have its advantages.

I could do a quick shop for ten items or less, fit them snugly inside the helmet, pop it on, and ride home like a low-budget courier.

The Scarecrow Biker

My mate Peter and I decided to have a night race down a country lane, Peter on his Suzuki TS50, me on the FS1E.

We tore through the darkness toward an imaginary finish line at the bottom of Penny Turnpike Hill, a steep descent that felt like the edge of the world.

I took the lead, twisted the throttle to full-blown wave, and surged ahead.

A glance at my right mirror revealed nothing but blackness, no sign of Peter's headlight.

Had I lost him already?

I must be travelling at the speed of light.

Wow, I thought. I've got the makings of the next World Superbike Champion.

Then I checked the left mirror, and, as if by magic, Peter's headlight appeared.

Unable to figure out the optical illusion, I fiddled with my crash helmet.

Mystery solved: the bloody thing had done its usual rotating act, limiting me to vision in just one eye.

I yanked the visor down.

Bloody rotating crash helmet.

Peter started disappearing again, this time in both mirrors.

Just before descending Penny Turnpike Hill, I checked once more. No sign of him.

I raced to the bottom, parked up, whipped off my helmet, and leaned smugly against the FS1E, channeling Marlon Brando's iconic biker pose.

After a few minutes waiting for "Mister Loser" to appear, concern crept in.

I instantly transformed from cool Brando into Lance Corporal Jones from *Dad's Army*:

"Don't panic! Don't panic!"

I jumped back on the FS1E and climbed Penny Turnpike Hill at a blistering 10 mph, on a search-and-rescue mission.

As I reached the crest, a dull light approached slowly. It was Peter.

We pulled into a nearby driveway.

His headlight was damaged, he'd clearly had an accident.

I pulled up alongside him.

As he turned to face me, my concern dissolved into uncontrollable laughter. His nose sported a lump of mud.

Branches, some still with leaves, poked out of his open-face crash helmet. He looked like Worzel Gummidge: the Scarecrow Stunt Rider.

Peter wasn't laughing. He looked horrified. After a couple of gulps, I managed to ask:

Me: "What the fuck happened to you?"

Peter: "I was trying my hardest to keep up, but you disappeared. I banked hard right into a sharp bend…

Turns out it wasn't a bend. It was a straight bit of road. I rode straight into the bloody hedgerow!"

Peter was well and truly distressed.

Meanwhile, I was discreetly rotating my helmet 180 degrees to hide my face as my concerned expression crumbled.

Eventually, the laughter overflowed.

My eyes watered.

Snot burst from my nose as I noticed both lenses on Peter's NHS black-rimmed glasses were cracked.

I knelt there for ten minutes, crippled by laughter, genuinely concerned I'd never breathe again.

The only real injury Peter suffered was to his pride.

He had one more minor accident before hanging up his crash helmet and retiring from mopeds for good.

Me?

I kept riding, one eye on the road, one eye on the shop windows.

Wheelie Inferno

Given my poor track record on one wheel, I eventually found a workaround that let me compete with Perry, *The Unicycle*.

I'd hoist the front wheel of my FS1E into the air, then drag my toes along the ground behind me, using them as stabilisers. I was a Wheelie Wizard.

Thankfully, my toes were protected by steel toe-cap boots. Anything less and I'd have been left with ten gurney-faced digits.

I'm not sure this technique complied with the rules and regulations of the Official Wheelie Foundation, but hey, I could stay up on one wheel for what felt like an eternity.

An eternity?

Well… not exactly.

The laws of friction had other plans.

"The heat generated when two surfaces rub against each other, causing a conversion of kinetic energy into thermal energy."

Translation: the smell of burning and my socks catching fire happened simultaneously.

After nearly completing a marathon on one wheel, my steel toe-cap riding boots, now worn down to the metal, were glowing red, trailing sparks behind me.

I looked like Sonic the Hedgehog.

Sitting on the pavement, trying to untie two laces at once, I discovered a hidden talent for panic-induced dexterity.

Holy mother of God!

Pulling my feet from the inferno inside those boots was like yanking marshmallows out of a fire pit.

My steel toe-cap riding boots, aka work safety boots, were now safety hazards.

Replacing them? Not easy.

I sat on the pavement, socks smouldering, wondering if the Official Wheelie Foundation offered compensation for third-degree stupidity.

I was on apprentice wages, juggling a dandelion and burdock pop addiction and a perpetually hungry petrol tank.

Financially, things were tight.

The next few months became a masterclass in creative budgeting… and literal freewheeling.

Interlude:

Just before the FS1E leaves the tale, here's a remarkably interesting fact:

In 1976, a brand-new Yamaha FS1E cost £236, and a brand-new Rolls-Royce cost £17,900.

In 2025, both are worth approximately £5,000.

So, to all you rich folk who bought a Rolls-Royce instead of a Yamaha FS1E in 1976:

You invested in the wrong vehicle!

Although, I can't quite picture Parker in a rotating crash helmet riding an FS1E and shouting, "Yes, M'Lady!", Lady Penelope snuggled up behind him.

Outerlude:

Where was I?…

Love at Full Throttle

Enter the other Pete, and his Kawasaki KH250.

A road bike dressed in stick-on plastic bits, desperately trying to pass as a single-seat competition racer. Fondly known as the Kawasaki *Mean Greenie*.

It looked and sounded like a race bike, all high-pitched ring-a-ding fury from its aggressive two-stroke engine. So loud, deaf people could hear it, while deafening everyone else.

The single-seat design didn't stop me from riding pillion. Pete and I were very close in those days.

Possibly too close.

He often remarked I was "a pain in the arse" whenever I clung to the back of his bike.

Physics agreed. Two people on a single-seat racer turned handling into a nightmare.

Pete, being a competent rider with a sadistic streak, never missed a chance to scare the snot out of me.

Unfortunately, sometimes the bike scared the snot out of Pete. Our lives were at risk on a weekly basis.

Once, while tearing down a side street, Pete went full throttle to impress two girls walking nearby. He was so focused on impressing them, he forgot about the Highway Code. And basic stopping distances.

As we passed, two things became clear:

1. We had their attention, confirmed by grimacing faces and fingers jammed in ears.

2. We had nowhere near enough road left before the junction with a busy main street.

Moments later, we were stopped dead in the middle of that main road, miraculously avoiding a bonnet-based death.

Another cat life wasted.

Fate was firmly on Pete's side that day. Not only did he survive, he ended up marrying one of those girls.

I, however, did not marry the other.

My crash helmet had rotated mid-ride, making it look like I was ignoring them entirely. The relationship was on the back foot before it had even begun.

In hindsight, that should've been the omen.

Ten years, two houses, ten acres, one cat, two dogs, four horses, and two cockatiels later, we finally admitted it was never going to last.

Who knows what might've happened if Pete had prioritised road safety over impressing the opposite sex?

One Wheel, One Dream, One Wrecked Ambition

Shortly after turning seventeen, I passed my motorbike test and part-exchanged my beloved FS1E for a Kawasaki KE175 scrambler.

The ideal machine for wheelies. Or so I thought.

Perry, of course, seamlessly transferred his one-wheel wizardry from stunt pushbike to motorbike, which pissed me off.

In the world of wheelies, Perry was the Bonnie Blue on a film set: flawless, tireless, and annoyingly photogenic.

I, on the other hand, was one of the many teenage virgins, over and done within seconds.

To extend my wheelie time, I needed to lift the front wheel in first gear, then smoothly shift into second, essential for longer one-wheel control.

But every time I made that gear change, the front wheel thudded back to Earth like a dropped anvil.

Would I ever earn my Wheelie Competency Badge?

Yes. Yes, I would.

In 1980, every Sunday morning, bikers would gather at Llandow's disused runway, a quarter-mile drag strip with no organisation, no rules, and no entry fee.

Just turn up and race.

The ambulance service considered it a dangerous pastime, so they were always there, just in case.

At one end of the runway was a shorter adjoining strip that doubled as a go-kart track and warm-up area, perfect for wheelie practice.

I began my quest there, away from the chaos, at the bottom of the short runway.

Again and again: first gear… second gear… thud. Failure was becoming a habit.

Then came the magic moment.

Riding toward the drag strip, I lifted the KE175 onto one wheel in first gear, opened the throttle, and kicked it into second.

WHOOSH!

No thud.

The front wheel climbed. Higher. Then higher. Then even higher.

A déjà vu moment, except this time it came with an engine and a death wish.

Suddenly, I was in uncharted territory, no clue how to stop the wheel's backwards journey.

I panicked.

Instinct took over.

I bailed, jumping off the back and letting the bike finish the wheelie solo.

I was going too fast to hit the ground running and survive, so I executed a Russian gymnast-style roly-poly, three perfect forward rolls, landing on my knees, facing my bike.

Just in time to witness the KE175 perform two spectacular sideways somersaults, bouncing high into the air before crashing back down in a heap of twisted metal.

Totally unhurt, I placed both hands on my crash helmet in disbelief at the carnage. Big mistake.

Beyond the wreckage, a crowd of bikers came rushing toward me, closely followed by an ambulance, sirens blazing.

I knew rotating my helmet 180 degrees to hide wouldn't help this time.

I leapt up, rushed to my mangled bike, and tried to drag it away from the scene.

The mob swarmed.

Questions flew from all directions.

Then, from the middle of the crowd, the Ambulance Man appeared.

Ambulance Man: "OK, everybody, stand back! Let me through."

Then, standing directly in front of me:

Ambulance Man: "What's your name?"

Me *(joking)*: "No! My name's not Watts!" (Nerves had triggered my comedy reflex.)

He shook his head.

Ambulance Man *(unamused)*: "How's your head?"

Me *(slightly confused)*: "What do you mean?"

Ambulance Man: "You were holding your head after coming off your bike."

Me: "I put my hands on my head in frustration, because my bike was trying to destroy itself, and I couldn't stop it."

Ambulance Man: "Are you hurt anywhere?"

Me: "Only my pride, it's killing me."

The biker mob groaned in unison, unleashing a Monty Python-esque sigh of disappointment. They wanted blood, and nothing but.

Disappointed, they turned and trudged back to the drag strip, followed by the first responders.

I gathered the scattered pieces of my bike, stuffed them into my jacket, hoisted the twisted KE175, and made my exit via the go-kart track, strategically avoiding the ride of shame past the mob and the humourless Ambulance Man.

My motorbiking days were officially numbered.

Once the KE175 was repaired, I placed an ad in the local paper.

With all the flair of a second-hand car salesman, I even included "careful owner" in the description.

Within a week, it was gone.

The new owner, clearly, hadn't witnessed the Llandow stunt spectacular.

It was time to move on… to four wheels.

Hopefully with more success, and a dash more street credibility.

Driving

Viva Las Chippenham

I started driving cars at the tender age of twelve.

Dad taught me, not to hire me out as child labour to a local taxi firm, but because he knew my number-one passion in life was cars.

On the occasional Sunday, he'd take me to a disused go-kart track, part of an old RAF base at Llandow. There, he taught me how to drive. Probably just as well the track was disused. A twelve-year-old perched on a height-enhancing cushion, piloting a Vauxhall Viva in the British Go-Kart Championship, would've violated every motorsport regulation ever written.

Sometimes I imagine myself standing alone on the winner's podium, hoisting the championship cup skyward, as ambulances whisk away my fellow competitors, aka Viva victims, to the nearest hospital.

Now, Dad's Vauxhall Viva may not have been the "must-have" car of the 1970s, but I adored it. It belonged to Vauxhall's no-frills range, so when we inevitably broke down, there were no extra knobs or fancy switches to distract us. We sat in silence on the hard shoulder, entertained only by the sound of passing traffic, the occasional wasp, and the flickering hope of an AA recovery truck.

My favourite Viva tale happened on the way home to Barry after a weekend at my uncle and auntie's place in Portsmouth.

Dad was working that weekend, so Mum had the pleasure of chauffeuring us in the ever-so-reliable Viva.

The first hour was uneventful. Then… things changed.

As we approached the Chippenham junction on the M4, we hit slow-moving traffic.

Interlude:

Now, slow traffic on UK motorways is standard. I'm convinced it's the Department of Transport's answer to overpopulation.

Here's the logic:

If half the population is stuck on the roads at any given time, towns and cities are only operating at 50 per cent capacity.

Problem solved. Genius.

But it doesn't stop there.

They've also introduced the 'Pothole Scheme', a clever initiative designed to keep even more people on the side of the road, countering the population boom caused by the English Channel dinghy contingency.

Who says road taxes aren't used wisely?

Outerlude:

Where was I…?

Road to Nowhere

The motorway under the Chippenham junction was blocked off due to roadworks. Cars were being diverted up the exit slip road and straight back down the entry road on the other side, bypassing the mess.

What the clever people at Roadworks HQ hadn't factored into their plan… was our Vauxhall Viva.

As we entered the exit road, the Viva decided to take a 'Nana Nap'.

We broke down. Right there. In the middle of the one-lane slip road.

Metal guardrail on one side, concrete blocks on the other. No room for the cars behind us to pass.

In front of us: clear road.

Behind us: the traffic jam from hell.

At one point, I think the Viva had more followers than the Kardashians.

With nowhere to go, a concerto of car horns filled the air. I took the opportunity to play *Name That Tune: Gridlock Edition*.

Mum, meanwhile, knew mobile phones wouldn't be invented for another fifteen years, so she rested her head on the steering wheel and decided to wait until they were.

Eventually, the cavalry arrived: two red-faced motorway cops in a patrol car, driving the wrong way down the slip road. Blue lights flashing, sirens screaming.

They pulled up in front of us and jumped out.

Policeman: "What's the problem, Madam?"

Mum: "I'm so sorry. The car won't start."

To prove her point, she turned the key. Nothing.

Policeman: "OK, we need to get you off this road. Can you open the bonnet? Might just be a loose wire."

Mum: "Um… how do I open the bonnet?"

Policeman: "Pull the bonnet release under the dashboard."

Mum: "Um…"

Policeman *(suspicious)*: "This is your car, Madam?"

Mum: "Yes, of course it is."

Policeman: "Can I see your driver's licence?"

Mum: "Yes… but it's at home."

Policeman *(sighing)***:** "You should always carry your driving licence. How do I know this is your car?"

Mum: "Because I'm driving it?"

The policeman let out a long, weary sigh.

Policeman *(now slightly frustrated)***:** "What's your registration number, Madam?"

Mum: "Pardon?"

Policeman: "Your number plate. What's on it?"

Mum: "Oh, that's easy."

She opened her door, gently nudged the officer aside, walked to the front of the car, and began pointing at each letter and number like she was teaching him to read.

Mum: "R… B… O… three… two… G."

The policeman looked up at the sky, searching for divine intervention.

Policeman *(bemused)***:** "There's no way anyone as innocent as you could've stolen this car."

"Get back in, we'll push you to the top of the road."

Policeman Two reversed the patrol car with practised ease. The bemused policeman, now flanked by a fluorescent workman and a hairy biker in leather, took position behind the Viva and began to push.

After a few yards, a voice yelled out:

Policeman *(breathless)***:** "Madam, have you still got the handbrake on?!"

Mum: "Um! Yes."

The breathless policeman suddenly became a ventriloquist, speaking through gritted teeth without moving his lips.

Policeman *(ventriloquist mode)*: "Madam… please take the handbrake off."

Mum: "Certainly."

She instantly released the handbrake. The car lurched forward. The three pushers, caught mid-thrust, crumpled like synchronised dominoes behind the boot.

As they stood up, their heads reappeared above the boot lid. The multi-talented policeman was now doing the opposite of ventriloquism, angrily mouthing words in silence, accompanied by sharp nods of the head.

He had the same skill set as Dad.

As I looked back at the scene, the policeman, the workman, the biker, I thought:

All we need now is the Lone Ranger and Tonto to turn up, and we've got a full Village People tribute band ready to belt out "Y.M.C.A."

Having done our bit for the Department of Transport by keeping even more people out of suburbia, we were dumped on the side of the road to wait for the AA breakdown service.

As we sat in the car, the multi-talented policeman drove past.

We gave him a fond farewell wave.

He responded with a vigorous wave of his own.

Me: "Mum… I didn't notice earlier that the policeman had three fingers missing?"

Practice Makes Panic

By the time I was fifteen, the Vauxhall Viva had evolved into an Opel Ascona, and I'd well and truly outgrown the go-kart track. I needed a new challenge to sharpen my driving skills.

So Dad never put L plates on the Ascona, and let me drive around the country roads anyway. Because that would've been illegal. Technically.

And it would've been just as illegal if he'd let me drive through Cardiff city centre at sixteen. Which, of course, he did, several times.

Miraculously, by the time I turned seventeen, I was more than ready for my driving test.

It had always been my dream to pass on my birthday.

Unfortunately, that didn't happen, thanks to a backlog of eager learners and a testing schedule that moved slower than a Morris Minor in second gear.

In the meantime, I booked a couple of lessons with a driving instructor, just to iron out a few "bad habits".

Personally, I didn't see a problem with:

- Tooting the horn to appreciate a good-looking girl
- Tailgating slow drivers to encourage them to hurry along
- Slamming on the brakes and screaming if passengers dared to close their eyes

All part of the joy of motoring, I thought.

And then, at last, the day of reckoning arrived.

The Test.

The plan was to have a calming lesson beforehand.

So much for planning.

There I was, on the day of my test, not in Dad's trusty Opel Ascona, but in a Ford Escort Mk1 I'd never driven before.

And next to me sat Mr *"If I had a personality, I wouldn't be doing this job"*, the dreaded Test Examiner.

Why wasn't I in the Ascona?

Because the night before, Mum took me out for a quick lesson. Everything was going fine until a sickly hot-water smell filled the car, followed by clouds of steam, or, as Mum called it, "fire and smoke".

The head gasket had blown.

I was now vehicle-less for my driving test.

To make matters worse, the only car I'd ever driven on the road was Dad's Opel Ascona.

So there I was: 9 pm, no plan, no hope, and a test booked for 10 am.

Test Day: Panic Mode

The next morning, I raced to the driving school's office on my motorbike. By 8:30 am, I was pacing outside like a man awaiting a verdict.

Then Pam, my instructor, appeared, on foot.

Pam: "You're a bit premature, Steve. Your lesson's not until nine."

This would not be the last time a woman told me I was a bit premature.

Me: "Pam! I haven't got a car for the lesson, or, more importantly, the test!"

I explained the whole sorry saga.

Pam: "The school car's out with John, the other instructor. He's not due back until eleven."

Me: "OMG. That's after my test!"

Pam: "Best go looking for John. He uses the same training routes as me, you might track him down."

I calmly jumped on my motorbike and took off at 100 mph.

After thirty minutes of frantic excursions around Barry Town, I spotted the driving school's one and only car.

It was mid-lesson.

To attract their attention, I did what any rational, desperate seventeen-year-old would do:

I overtook the car, slammed on the brakes, and pulled up sharply in front, forcing the poor learner to test their emergency-stop skills.

Lucky for me, their skills were test-ready.

With a lot of pleading, more like full-blown begging, I managed to commandeer the driving school's vehicle for my test.

At 9:55 am, outside the Test Centre, I was presented with their old faithful Ford Escort.

I jumped into the driver's seat … and froze.

The visibility in the Escort was more Panzer tank than the goldfish-bowl clarity of our beloved Ascona.

At that moment, I found myself desperately wishing Field Marshal Willie Schnapper would appear to offer some last-minute tank-driving tips.

Instead, the door of the tank creaked open, and in climbed Mr Frosty the Examiner, clipboard in hand, personality left at home.

As he fastened his seatbelt, he barked:

Mr Frosty: "Rank, name, and number?"

I handed over my correctly folded paper provisional licence.

Interlude:

For those unfamiliar with the old-school paper licence, it wasn't like today's sleek, credit-card-style version.

No, this was a full-blown paper database. It held everything:

- Driving endorsements
- Date of birth
- Dietary requirements
- Name of your first girlfriend

Unfold it fully, and you could wallpaper a small lounge.

Fold it back? Impossible.

If that had been part of the test, we'd all still be riding pushbikes.

It was harder than a Rubik's Cube dipped in glue.

Outerlude:

Where was I…?

Final Checks Before Take-Off

Satisfied with my credentials, Mr Frosty gave me the rundown of what I could and couldn't do during the test.

Mr Frosty: "No tooting at pretty girls. You may slam on the brakes, but only if I nod off and my clipboard hits my knees."

I took a deep breath.

And we were off.

The Checklist

I ran through everything Pam had drilled into me:

1. Exaggerate your head movements.

So the examiner knows you're checking your mirrors.

For the past month, I'd been walking around like a dashboard bobblehead.

I'd become so addicted to the motion, I looked like a puppet from *Thunderbirds*.

2. Mirror – Signal – Manoeuvre.

I'd been practising this routine in discos for years:

- **Mirror**, Make sure I look irresistible.

- **Signal**, Make eye contact with a chick.

- **Manoeuvre**, Make my move.

Sadly, this had never resulted in a successful coupling.

Today, the circumstances were slightly different.

And Mr Frosty had clearly taken his ugly pills, so there was no risk of romantic confusion.

3. Know your stopping distances.

Now, I don't know if anyone else noticed, but back in the day the Highway Code only showed stopping distances from a side view.

How does that work?

Here's the scenario:

I'm stopped at a T-junction in a 30 mph zone. Suddenly, Aunty Mary drives by.

My mathematical mind, fuelled by Pythagoras's Serum, instantly calculates that she was within the 21-metre danger zone of the car in front.

A clear violation of the sacred Code of Safe Stopping Distances.

In a panic, I phone her.

Me: "Aunty Mary! You're in imminent danger! You're too close to the car in front, for God's sake, back off!"

Aunty Mary: "How do you propose I do that? The car in front is your Uncle Derek. He's towing me to the garage to get my car fixed!"

Back to the test.

Not many people can say they passed their driving test in a German military vehicle. But somehow, I did.

Field Marshal Willie Schnapper would've been proud.

I imagined him saluting me:

Willie Schnapper: "Vell done, you Velsh Vanker."

And with that, licence in hand, I officially earned the right to become…

A Boy Racer.

All I needed now was a race car.

The Exhausted Showman

Enter: my 1969 Ford Cortina 1600E.

Coincidentally, the same model as Jeremy Clarkson's first car, though I'm not sure his came with the same optional extras.

Mine had a detachable gearstick.

And a detachable exhaust.

Let's start with the gearstick.

I first discovered this 'feature' at a set of lights, pulled up next to a bright red, sporty-looking Mini. The lights turned green. Game on.

A little squeal from the rear tyres as I surged ahead.

The Mini fell behind.

To keep the momentum, I went for an ultra-quick change into second.

Instead of second gear, I found myself waving goodbye, with the gearstick in my hand.

As the little old lady in the bright red, sporty-looking Mini calmly undertook me, completely unaware she'd just won a drag race.

Then there was the exhaust.

That particular 'option' revealed itself one sunny afternoon outside a very busy pub.

The beer garden was buzzing. A few of my mates were there, along with a generous helping of strangers.

As I left the car park, my friends egged me on to perform one of my legendary wheel spins.

Not one to disappoint, I let rip.

But instead of tyre smoke and screeching glory, the Cortina decided to impersonate a building-site dump truck.

The back box of the exhaust system had come apart.

Embarrassing enough?

Not quite.

The back box didn't just fall off, it lodged itself into the tarmac, stopping the car dead.

There I was, stuck in place, engine roaring, going nowhere.

I had no choice but to perform emergency repairs, flat on my back, on the tarmac, in front of a full beer garden.

They were full of drink.

And full of forgiveness.

Well… full of drink, anyway.

I could've charged for the entertainment.

I don't think any stand-up comedian in history has endured the level of heckling I received that sunny afternoon.

It was clear: the Cortina 1600E had served its purpose. It was time to transition to my next vehicle.

Unfortunately… that transition didn't go according to plan.

Cops and Dodgers

I swapped my Cortina 1600E for a Cortina Mk3 GT.

The transaction was simple: a handshake and a key swap. No money. No paperwork. No questions asked.

It was a Friday afternoon.

I spent the next 24 hours driving around town in what would become my favourite car ever.

Eventually, late on Saturday night, I parked the Cortina outside my house, exhausted but elated. I went inside, grabbed the food Mum had left out, and collapsed on the settee, fully clothed, full of chips, and fighting off driver fatigue.

Then, on the stroke of midnight, I was woken by flashing blue lights outside the house.

I leapt to my feet, assuming the neighbours had been up to no good.

Before I could reach the window, Phil Collins started drumming on our front door.

Oh, shite.

This didn't sound good.

I opened the door to find an angry policeman, backed up by four others.

PC Angry: "Are you Steven Michael Rowley?"

Uh-oh.

He'd used my full name, including the middle one.

That's never a good sign.

Me: "Yes?"

PC Angry: "Are you the owner of a Ford Cortina, registration blah blah blah?"

In full panic mode, I only heard the words *Ford Cortina*.

Me: "Yes."

The long arm of the law reached out and grabbed my arm, just as Mum appeared like a superhero in slippers.

Mum: "Oh my God! What's going on?"

PC Angry: "Steven has just been involved in a car chase and fled the scene."

Me *(protesting)*: "What?! No, I haven't! I've got no idea what you're talking about!"

PC Angry: "We were chasing your Ford Cortina before you abandoned it and fled on foot."

Suddenly, I wasn't worried about being arrested, I was more worried about my car.

Me: "Wait… are you telling me my car's been stolen?!"

PC Angry: "No. I'm telling you your car was just involved in a police chase."

Mum *(alibi mode)*: "But I heard him pull up just before you got here, officer."

PC Angry: "Oh no you didn't."

Mum: "Oh yes I did."

The situation was rapidly turning into a pantomime.

Then I noticed something that changed everything.

Me: "My car is behind you."

PC Angry: "This is no time for games. You're coming with us."

He started pulling my arm.

Me: "No, no! My car really is behind you!"

I pointed past the Keystone Cops to my shiny Ford Cortina GT.

Me: "There's my car."

PC Angry: "Oh no it's not."

Me: "Oh yes it is."

We were now fully committed to the pantomime theme.

PC Angry: "That's not the car we were chasing. It was your Cortina 1600E registered to you."

Me: "But I swapped it yesterday, for that car."

(Still pointing at my Cortina GT.)

Then the penny dropped, loudly, like a Cortina exhaust hitting tarmac.

The guy I'd swapped cars with… was the escapee.

Eventually, Mum and I convinced PC Angry that the car in the chase was no longer mine.

I gave them the address of the new owner of the Cortina 1600E.

After a stern lecture about not having receipts, PC Angry and the Keystone Cops left to track down the real culprit.

One Week Later…

I ran into the guy I'd swapped cars with.

Me: "What happened with the police chase?"

Escapee *(reliving his glory)***:**

"The cops started chasing me, no insurance, so I thought, *'Right, time to go full Fast & Furious.'*

I floor it. I'm flying, adrenaline pumping… until the gear stick comes off in my hand.

So I bail, ditch the car, and, get this, I report it stolen."

I gave him a cheeky grin.

Me: "You were lucky the exhaust didn't fall off."

Escapee: "It did. That's why they were chasing me. It sounded like a building-site dump truck."

Repairs and Regrets

Maintaining my Cortina GT became so costly that most of the replacement parts were second-hand, or, as I preferred to call them, *"nearly old."*

One day, I mentioned to my mate Andrew that the rear axle was knackered.

Driving it felt like sitting on a washing machine loaded with bedding on full spin.

It might've been a go-to optional extra for the lonely housewife, but it wasn't doing my racing career any favours.

Andrew: "I know where there's an abandoned Cortina. The bloke who owned it parked it on some waste ground outside our workshop and buggered off overseas."

Abandoned Cortina.

That sounded exactly like my price range.

So Pete and I spent an entire weekend removing and replacing axles.

By late Sunday, everything was bolted back into place.

Time for a test run.

Success.

Full-load fast spin eliminated.

Normal service resumed.

But Wait… There's More

A few months later, Pete needed a part for his little Triumph Spitfire.

He found what he was after at the local car wrecker's yard, but was struggling to remove it.

Then a stranger appeared.

Helpful Guy: "Need a hand, mate?"

Pete: "If you don't mind, that'd be great."

Together, they got the part off. Pete, ever the gentleman, felt indebted.

Pete: "Thanks, mate. I don't think I could've done that without you."

Helpful Guy: "No problem. Glad to help."

Pete: "What are you here for? Can I give you a hand?"

Helpful Guy: "Nah, I've already got what I came for."

Pete: "What did you come to get?"

Helpful Guy: "A bloody axle for my Cortina! Some lowlife nicked it while I was away at sea for a couple of months."

Pete *(in shock)*: "Bastards! Where was it parked?"

The bloke described, in perfect detail, the exact spot where Pete and I had spent a weekend lovingly *"rescuing"* an axle.

Helpful Guy: "If I find them, I'll break their bloody necks."

Pete: "Oh! Maybe they just thought the car was abandoned? Anyway, I probably wouldn't have been much help to you today, I've never removed an axle before in my life."

After an awkward pause:

Pete: "Must dash, someone's '10-4 Rubber Ducking' me on my CB radio."

Helpful Guy looked utterly baffled, his expression frozen as if he'd just been Tango'd.

Pete paid for his parts, waited in the office until Mr Helpful Guy was out of sight, then sprinted to his car and disappeared into the sunset.

Interlude:

You've Been Tango'd was a British TV advertising campaign for a fizzy orange drink, featuring a deranged Orange Man who would materialise from nowhere and deliver a double-handed slap to the face of the victim after taking a slurp of their drink, an aggressive metaphor for "refreshing taste".

I often wonder if President Trump modelled his entire persona on this character: appearing out of nowhere to slap world leaders with a booming,

"You've Been Tariff'd!"

Outerlude:

Where was I?…

Parting ways with my Cortina GT was just as eventful, a snapped ignition key, slipping clutch, and a mismatched passenger door in a very wrong shade.

But that, dear reader, is a tale for another time.

Nightclubbing at the Disco

Discoing for Beginners

When did going to the disco become nightclubbing?

Probably around the same time dinner time at school was renamed lunchtime, and dinner ladies were quietly phased out, replaced by vending machines that classed crisps as a nutritionally balanced lunch alternative.

Progress? Not in my world.

I miss the hairnets.

And I miss the mash.

Sugar Dust Contraceptives

Nightclubbing for me kicked off at The Fantasia "Disco", an underwater-themed venue tucked away at the bottom of the road leading to Barry Island.

Locals affectionately dubbed it "The Fanny", which made everything sound a touch more scandalous than it probably was.

Interlude:

One Saturday, while browsing the high street, a hand clamped onto my shoulder and spun me around like I'd just been drafted.

Christ, it was Vinnie.

Boxing champ. Built like a fridge. Not a man you disagreed with for sport.

Vinnie: "Mister Rowley! I want you to go in there", he jabbed a finger towards the chemist shop, "and buy me a packet of dunkies (Barry speak for condoms). I'm going down The Fanny tonight and feel lucky."

Me: "You've got to be joking, Vinnie! No way I'm buying dunkies for you. Too embarrassing!"

Two minutes later, I handed him the dunkies and his change.

Don't get me wrong, I actually got on really well with Vinnie, although he once caused me to have an actual out-of-body experience during a sparring session at the local boxing club.

I don't remember the punch.

I do remember standing in the ring, arms limp at my sides, staring blankly and wondering:

"What the hell are all these people doing in my bedroom?"

I was promptly escorted from the ring, in a noble attempt to be reunited with my marbles.

Two butterfly stitches later, I retired from the sport.

Dunkies, a.k.a. condoms, actually triggered a bizarre addiction to Dextrol Energy lozenges.

I kept failing to buy what I actually needed in chemists, because every time I tried to say "condoms", I'd panic and default to:

Me: "A pack of com… com, Dextrols, please. Blackcurrant."

It became my signature cocktail of embarrassment: one part flustered mumble, one part fruity lozenge.

It escalated quickly.

I was downing them by the handful, so wired some nights I couldn't sleep, vibrating like a faulty fridge.

One particularly intense week, I didn't sleep at all. My body ran entirely on panic and blackcurrant sugar dust.

Outerlude:

Where was I?…

Chicks, Mints and Pigeons

I was sixteen when I first infiltrated The Fantasia.

My sister knew the doorman, Austin Martin, no less, which meant Perry and I slipped past security into The Fanny.

Disco by name. Misadventure by nature.

Dad agreed to let me go under strict conditions:

• My sister had to be there.

• He'd pick us up at the end of the night.

• And the big one, no drinking.

I promised faithfully not to drink.

So naturally, the moment I got inside, I headed straight to the bar and bought my first pint, confident the pack of extra-strong mints stuffed in my pocket would mask the effects (and odour) of alcohol when Dad picked us up.

All part of the master plan to appear stone-cold sober.

The plan? Genius.

The execution? Debatable.

By 11:30 p.m., I'd asked ten girls to dance.

Twelve said no.

Two rejected me pre-emptively, before I'd even opened my mouth.

As the end of my first night at The Fanny loomed, a sudden thought struck me:

Where's Perry?

I'd already gone full Godfather, half a pack of extra-strong mints stuffed in my mouth.

All I had to do now was insert the remaining half into Perry's.

But he was nowhere to be seen.

That night, I explored every inch of The Fanny.

No matter how hard I tried, I couldn't find the right spot.

Perry had gone AWOL.

On my second sweep of the men's toilet, I clocked one cubicle door, still shut, just as it had been when my search began.

Surely not…

I knocked.

No reply.

Dad was waiting outside, and I knew if I wasn't there on time, he'd come marching in, drag me out by the ear.

Right past all the girls who'd rejected me as a dance partner.

Definitely not the John Travolta exit I'd had in mind.

Panicking, and with no other option, I pushed the cubicle door open,

And there he was.

Hugging the toilet seat like he'd just proposed to it.

Me: "For fuck's sake, Perry!"

Perry *(slurring)*: "Ugggh… I drank too much."

I had no choice but to prematurely end Perry's intimate relationship with the toilet seat.

I dragged him to his feet and, with the sleight of a magician's hand, deposited the remaining mints into his mouth.

Now I was face-to-face with Perry, attempting to communicate with this Neanderthal.

Me *(talking slowly)*: "My dad's outside. He'll kill me if he knows we've been drinking, so act normal."

Perry nodded, pretending to understand.

Then belched in my face.

It's hard to describe the effect of a cocktail of alcohol and extra-strong mints being blasted into your face at close range.

All I can say is, I'm glad I wasn't smoking.

I imagined a spontaneous explosion, then emerging with no eyebrows, a blackened face, and smoke gently rising from my hair as I trudged towards Dad.

"Hi, Dad! Told you I'd be OK!"

Partially blinded by Perry's aromatic mouth-fragrance, I fumbled my way around The Fanny, dragging him behind me, until we found the exit.

Outside was Dad, sitting patiently in his car.

As we walked towards him, I gave an enthusiastic wave, as if to say, *Look at me, Dad! I'm safe and sober!*

Unfortunately, the delinquent chimp I was dragging behind me gave the game away.

I think Dad was just relieved I'd survived and was still intact.

No interrogation.

No mention of our mint-inspired Godfather impersonations.

We got into Dad's car and headed towards the zoo to drop off the chimp in the back seat… who was deteriorating by the minute.

Dad and I opened every window as Perry, no longer content with flammable mint breath, started releasing flammable gases from other regions of his anatomy.

It was an eye-watering journey back to Perry's house, and such a relief to offload him into the arms of his loving mother.

Well… sort of.

What actually happened was, I dragged the even-more-delinquent chimp to his front door, rang the bell, then jumped back into the car.

Just as the front door opened, I turned to Dad.

Me: "Go! Go! Go!"

Then, with a screech of tyres, Dad and I were,

Gone. Gone. Gone.

The next day, I visited the delinquent chimp, and was surprised to find Perry instead. A little worse for wear, but now coherent.

His mum's partner, Mike, asked what the hell I'd done to Perry before dumping him on the front step.

Me: "Not my fault, Mike! I was being rejected by numerous girls while Perry did his own thing!"

Mike: "When I opened the door after you dumped him on the step… things were happening at both ends of Perry. There was no way he was coming into the house in that state. He slept in the pigeon coop."

Me: "How are the pigeons?"

Mike: "I don't think they're homing pigeons anymore. After spending a night with Perry, next time they're released, it'll be a one-way ticket."

Karma Wears Beer Goggles

The Fanny on New Year's Eve was the place to be.

The party atmosphere was pumping, with every unattached male Singlette scouting for a female Singlette to share a midnight kiss.

It was snog mania on the dance floor.

I'd been dancing with a female Singlette when Big Ben began banging his gong.

By then, I was fully in the party spirit, and ended up snogging my dance partner.

The New Year had started well, so I seized the moment and walked her home.

Once outside, the fresh air began to sober me up, and by the time we reached her house, I was fully sober… and realised I'd made a mistake.

She was a lovely girl.

But with my beer goggles off, I knew I'd picked up the wrong keys from the ashtray.

I made a polite excuse to leave, shook hands, wished her a Happy New Year, then disappeared without looking back.

The following week at The Fanny, I was doing a stellar job of avoiding her, making it abundantly clear I had no interest in a relationship.

Just as I was about to leave, she came rushing up to me with a big smile on her face.

Beer Goggle Chick: "Don't bother speaking to me then."

Clearly, my ignoring strategy wasn't working.

Me: "That's a great idea."

Then I turned and vanished into the distance.

Not the kindest way to let someone down… but it worked.

Actually, if I'm honest - it was a bit spiteful.

Interlude:

And as we all know - karma never forgets.

Many, many, many years later, I attended my daughter's first gymnastics grading at the local YMCA.

I'd finished work and headed over for the event.

My wife was having a coffee, or should I say, a skinny flat white, extra hot, with a group of mothers.

Em: "You made it on time then!"

Me *(cheeky chappie mode)*: "You know me! I always arrive early."

Em: "You are so not funny."

Then she tapped her friend on the shoulder, who was facing the other way.

As she turned around,

Em: "This is my husband, Steve. Steve, this is my friend… Florence."

Holy mother of God.

It was New Year's Eve Beer Goggle Chick.

Our eyes met.

Obviously not for the first time. And we both knew it.

Me: "Hello, nice to meet you… for the first time."

Em *(confused)*: "What?"

Flo: "Oh! Nice to meet you, your face looks familiar."

Em, thinking she'd missed the joke, gave a faint, false laugh and continued with her coffee.

Me: "Right then! Uh… best I go find Megz and wish her good luck for her grading."

I spun around, desperate to escape this excruciatingly awkward moment, and headed towards the nearest door.

Unfortunately… the lost property cupboard, clearly labelled, was locked.

After a few frantic tugs on the handle, I had no choice but to turn around and walk past Em and Flo…

Towards the actual exit.

My impromptu comedy door routine caused Em to choke on her coffee. She looked at me in disbelief:

Em *(mouthing silently)*: "What the fuck?"

Me: "I was checking to see if my marbles were in there."

Totally flustered and red-faced, I left through the correct door.

The final image burned into my brain:

My wife, shaking her head in bewilderment, apologising for my comedy act…

And Flo, with the biggest grin you've ever seen.

Outerlude:

Where was I…?

Divine intervention - Chuckle Brother style

Back to The Fanny.

On another occasion, I wasn't having much success on the dance floor, basically, a standard night at The Fanny.

Then it happened … like the parting of the waves.

A gap opened through the crowded bar area onto the dance floor.

And there she was, an angel sent from heaven.

A blinding light from above shone down on her beautiful, long blonde hair.

A biblical moment.

Mesmerised by this vision of beauty, I turned to Pete, standing beside me, and asked him to pinch me, just to make sure I wasn't dreaming.

Pete: "What? Pinch you? I'm not that bloody drunk."

Fact:

The parting of the waves was actually caused by Austin Martin and a couple of doormen charging through the bar, trying to break up two lads fighting behind the Fantasia Angel.

The blinding light from above? The DJ's security floodlight, used to signal trouble on the dance floor.

The Fantasia Angel was dancing with her friend, who had their back to us, and also had beautiful, long blonde hair.

I turned to Pete.

Me: "Two blonde chicks at ten o'clock. Put your pint down, I need a wingman."

Pete dutifully followed me onto the dance floor.

Completely ignoring her dance partner, I stepped in front of the Fantasia Angel and asked her for a dance.

She didn't reply or bolt, so I figured my luck had finally turned.

Pete pirouetted to face her friend, who was behind me, and launched into his signature dance moves.

Now came the charm offensive.

First impressions are make-or-break on the dance floor, and I wasn't about to waste this golden opportunity.

In my head, I quickly rehearsed a couple of one-liners:

"Does heaven know they're missing an angel?" or

"You could've been a twin, because you're pretty enough for two."

I took a deep breath, leaned forward **towards** the Fantasia Angel,

Me: "Hi."

Oh my God.

My mouth and brain were clearly on different buses.

"Hi"?

That was it?

Definitely not what I'd planned.

I stopped myself just in time from delivering my next line, knowing full well she had zero interest in the weather.

Desperately trying to reunite my mouth and brain at the bus depot, I noticed her staring at me.

Not in a *"My God, you're gorgeous"* kind of way, more of a *"Please don't shoot me."*

I kept dancing, but things got stranger.

Her moves began to slow, causing mine to slow too, until we resembled two people in a busy street awkwardly blocking each other's path.

Only this wasn't a busy street.

Something wasn't right.

I glanced at Pete, and to my horror, he was wearing the exact same stare as the Fantasia Angel.

Now I was really starting to worry.

It felt like a scene from *The World's End*, not knowing who was human and who was an alien zombie.

I looked back at the Fantasia Angel.

Then back at Pete.

Yep, same stare.

I turned slightly and pinched Pete to get his attention.

This pinching thing between Pete and me was starting to become a worrying feature of our friendship.

He turned to look at me, no change of expression, then gave a short, sharp nod towards something in front of him and behind me.

Me *(mouthing silently)***:** "What?"

Pete's eyebrows, now touching his scalp, repeated the gesture with more vigour.

Not sure what I was about to witness, I slowly turned towards Pete's dance partner, half expecting two boyfriends to be standing either side of her, eyes laser-locked on the back of my head in full battle mode.

Nope.

Worse.

The Fantasia Angel and Pete's dance partner was … a Jesus Christ lookalike.

Long blonde hair, with a matching blonde beard and moustache.

JC and I exchanged smiles of awkwardness.

For a brief moment, I considered asking, *"Why do YOU think your dad let me poo my pants on the way home from infant school?"*

But I let it go.

Another missed opportunity.

I looked back at Pete.

Now my eyebrows touched my scalp.

Not sure how to resolve this embarrassing calamity, I turned back to the Fantasia Angel and leaned forward to apologise.

Me: "Bloody miserable weather we're having at the moment …"

Meanwhile, the four of us were still zombie dancing.

And continued to do so until I grabbed the traumatised Pete by the arm and dragged him off the dance floor, leading to the walk of shame through a crowd of clapping spectators, enjoying our accidental comedy sketch.

To this day, I still feel guilty for what we did that night.

Poor JC had taken one of his angels out for a quiet night, until the Chuckle Brothers gate-crashed their biblical evening.

My wife often refers to me as an **ACTUAL TWAT**.

I assume it's a term of endearment.

To finish:

I can't ever remember saying, *"I'm going down The Fantasia."*

It was always, *"I'm going down The Fanny."*

Had it been built at the top of the road, I probably would've said,

"I'm going up The ... Fantasia?"

It's all about context.

Steve Rowley

Maturing at the Cherry Pop Golf Club

Small Balls and Long Shafts

For me, my journey to manhood was somewhat complex and eventful.

There are many ways to describe losing one's virginity.

I've chosen an interesting analogy to describe my journey … a game of golf.

So, ladies and gentlemen, please return to your seats, place your tray tables in the upright position, and fasten your seatbelts, we're in for a bumpy ride.

For the slightly innocent among you, "popping the cherry" is a well-known euphemism for losing one's virginity.

The Cherry Pop Golf Club is unlike any other golf club.

The course has it all:

• The Tee (nerves and anticipation)

• The Fairway (hazards, detours, and the occasional lost ball)

• And finally, the Green, home of the Holy Grail for any teenage boy:

the place where the flag lives.

Or, as it shall now be known: **The Flag Home.**

Once you've played there, you become a lifelong member …

but you can never play there again.

WOW.

That sounds like the plot of J.K. Rowling's next book:

Harry Potter and the Lost Cherry.

There's one strict rule at the Cherry Pop Golf Club:

No one under the age of teenager is allowed.

The Car Park Years

So, my journey begins, appropriately, in the car park.

At the tender age of seven, I had my first girlfriend: Daryl Jones.

That's the age where holding hands is gross, kissing is yuk, and romance is defined by proximity and confectionery.

There were no prenuptial agreements.

Just two kids sitting on the sofa, sharing a pack of Jelly Tots and watching *Sesame Street*.

It was bliss.

But, as in every relationship, cracks began to form.

There were arguments, mostly about the naming of our future children.

I was happy with names like 1, 2, and 3, simple, efficient, easy to remember.

But no.

Daryl wanted Bert, Ernie, and Kermit.

The tension built, and eventually, it all came to a head one day at school …

Whilst I was deep in battle, playing Cowboys and Indians in the schoolyard, the call rang out that could stop any war in its tracks:

"Kiss Catch!"

The sacred ritual began when a group of girls, huddled in a circle like a coven of giggling witches, selected one of their own to become the Kiss Catchie.

On the call, the chosen girl would sprint like the clappers towards the sanctuary of the girls' toilets, while every boy in earshot dropped whatever he was doing and gave chase.

If caught, the Kiss Catchie had to kiss her way out of trouble, one quick peck on the cheek per captor.

I'd missed the initial call, as I was crouched behind the dustbins, reloading my imaginary rifle.

Suddenly, the arrows fell silent.

The schoolyard had gone eerily quiet at my end.

I popped my head up to survey the scene.

There she was,

I caught a glimpse of the back of the Kiss Catchie, disappearing down the side of the caretaker's shed, trailed by a stampede of Cowboys and Indians.

Curiosity got the better of me.

I skipped over and joined the end of the queue.

Nervously, I glanced around to make sure Daryl wasn't in sight.

The Floating Frog

As I waited my turn, I could hear the Kiss Catchie vetting her suitors:

• "Not you, you're ugly."

• "OK, I'll kiss you."

• "Not you, your nose is running."

It was nearly my moment.

Only the conjoined brothers, Colin and Brian, stood between me and my first kiss.

The tension between them was palpable, probably because one had been picked as a Cowboy and the other an Indian.

Sibling rivalry meets tribal warfare.

When their turn came, the Kiss Catchie sensed the tension, and rejected them both on the spot.

No hesitation.

No explanation.

Just a flat-out refusal.

Then, from nowhere, I heard a familiar voice:

"Steve, what are you doing here?"

Oh.

My.

God.

Daryl.

I froze.

I thought she'd crept up behind me, caught red-handed in a compromising queue of betrayal.

I turned around, sheepishly, bracing for the wrath of hell.

But … no one was there.

I turned back just as the conjoined twins shuffled off, still arguing.

And that's when my heart sank.

It was Daryl, she was the Kiss Catchie.

In a fit of temper, I reached into my pocket, pulled out my bag of Jelly Tots, and threw them at her feet.

Our relationship was over.

I know some of you reading this will have your own take on the situation, debating who was right, who was wrong, and whether Jelly Tots should ever be weaponised in a breakup.

But at the end of the day, I found myself single once again.

I turned to drink to help me get through this difficult stage in life and quickly became addicted to Corona Dandelion and Burdock pop.

My drinking habit inevitably led me down the path of crime.

I discovered a loophole in the money-back-on-empties scheme at the local grocery shop.

Here's how it worked:

Step 1: Return empty bottles to the shop.

Step 2: Receive 5p per bottle.

Step 3: Race around to the back lane.

Step 4: Wait for the shopkeeper to place the bottles back in the crate.

Step 5: Reunite myself with said bottles.

Step 6: Wait a respectful amount of time.

Step 7: Return to the front of the shop.

Step 8: Exchange the bottles for cash.

Again.

It was a perfect system.

I was essentially laundering glass.

The money funded my fizzy habit.

I was hooked.

Even at that age, I knew something had to change.

With the threat of my dad finding out about my crimes, and potentially chopping my fingers off for stealing, life had reached a turning point.

This was the 1960s.

Parents could get away with this type of punishment, and no one batted an eye.

Interlude:

I can only ever remember my dad smacking me once.

At the time, I thought he completely overreacted, he'd caught me playing chicken on the main road at the bottom of our street.

I'd dart across the road in front of oncoming cars, testing how close I could get without being run over … and maimed for life.

Unfortunately, my dad didn't share that thrill.

I found out when I unknowingly sprinted in front of his car.

He parked, got out, and escorted me across the road (when there were no cars coming, naturally).

Then he introduced me to moonwalking, not the Michael Jackson version that appears later in the tale, but the Neil Armstrong one.

I covered the 50-metre journey to our house in less than ten strides.

Dad's magical swings of his arm enabled me to defy gravity.

Lesson learnt!

My mum, on the other hand, had a unique style of punishment.

When I was being naughty and wouldn't stop, she'd give me a clip around the ear.

When I say "clip", it was more of a gentle rustle of my hair.

And then, ten minutes later, racked with guilt, she'd offer a peace treaty.

Once, she even bought me a pushbike: **The Golden Arrow**.

Dad discovered the peace offering when he drove past us in the park after a double back shift.

We waved enthusiastically to get his attention.

As soon as he saw the bike, he launched into his infamous routine, silently mouthing angry words, punctuated by short, sharp nods of disapproval.

Each nod confirmed his utter disgust at Mum's latest act of monetary recklessness.

Luckily for me, Mum always had the final word in the household.

So I kept my pride and joy: **The Golden Arrow**.

Now, some of you are probably thinking Mum was too soft.

Spoilt brat, some may say.

But no, **NEVER, EVER, EVER** doubt your mother's child psychology abilities.

From that day on, if I misbehaved, Mum would threaten me with a bike ban.

It became her ace card.

It worked every time.

Outerlude:

Where was I? …

Back to my life of crime.

Whilst sipping Dandelion and Burdock in the local park, I had a long, honest chat with myself and decided …

crime doesn't pay, especially if you're caught.

Deep down, I knew there was someone else out there, someone with whom I could share my Jelly Tots.

So, two days after the Kiss Catch ordeal, I was back to my old self.

My primary school love life after that incident was non-eventful, although, at one point, I did manage to have three non-contact girlfriends in one day!

Pretty cool, I thought at the time.

Unfortunately, due to a slight oversight, I lost all of them within the hour.

Michelle, Karen, and Carmilla were best friends, so keeping our individual relationships secret proved impossible.

Another lesson learnt.

Never date best friends.

Especially not simultaneously.

The Dyson Vacuum Discovery

My time in the golf club car park came to an end; it was time to play a round of golf at the Cherry Pop Golf Club.

At the age of thirteen, I entered the Cherry Pop Golf Club with excitement and great expectations, anticipating what was in store for me.

Feeling I had to be one step ahead of the game, I'd been secretly practising grown-up kissing, technically known as snogging.

Unfortunately, eBay didn't exist, so I couldn't purchase a Real Rita Chinese blow-up girlfriend to practise on.

The next best thing available … was my pillow.

I tried to emulate the technique of my favourite movie star, James Bond, mimicking the kisses he used on Bond girls.

I quickly discovered that a pillow was probably not the best substitute.

My practice sessions usually ended with me choking on a feather or two, made worse by the fact that the material soaked up all my saliva, leaving me with a dry cough.

Concerned by this mysterious cough, Mum would often say, "That doesn't sound right ... you're not going to school tomorrow."

As they say, *every cloud has a silver lining.*

Before I headed to the tee, I decided to have a couple of practice strokes ...

Well, to be honest, lots and lots of practice strokes.

Practice makes perfect!

I placed my ball on the tee.

Just the fairway between me and a boy's ultimate conquest, the first Flag Home.

I took a deep breath, firmly gripped the shaft of my wood, and swung it in the direction of the Flag Home.

My ball took flight, but I'd sliced it into the rough.

From that moment, I knew my journey along the fairway was going to have its ups and downs.

My first shot landed at the feet of Zoe.

While I was on holidays at my auntie's house in Portsmouth, I became friendly with the girl next door.

Zoe was about the same age and quite shy.

One day, we were sitting alone in her garden having a quiet chat, when I nervously brought up the subject of grown-up kissing.

She was extremely interested.

I asked if she'd ever kissed a boy before.

She hadn't.

So, I politely offered to demonstrate.

She accepted.

We gently kissed.

Then paused.

Me: "Did you like it?"

Zoe *(shyly)*: "Yes."

Feeling proud of my James Bond technique, I asked,

Me: "Shall we do it again?"

Zoe *(enthusiastically)*: "Yes please!"

We kissed again, but this time, I must've pressed the right button … because she suddenly turned into a Dyson vacuum cleaner.

I'm fairly certain Zoe must've been a pearl diver in a former life, how else could she hold her breath for so long?

Meanwhile, on my side of the kiss, I was running out of oxygen, drifting in and out of consciousness.

Then I heard her mum call out:

Zoe's Mum: "Zoe. Dinner."

Zoe quickly released me from the vacuum.

Zoe *(loudly)*: "I'm coming!"

Panicked, I managed a whisper:

Me: "For Christ's sake, don't tell your mother that! She'll kill me."

Then I collapsed onto the lawn, gasping for oxygen.

Zoe, God bless her, placed me in the recovery position, then disappeared into the house for dinner.

We never got another chance to perfect our snogging skills.

Our brief holiday romance was over before it truly began.

One Kiss, Two Eyes and The Wrong Mother

My second shot landed at Michelle's feet.

By the time I got to Michelle, I was fifteen.

We met at The Knap Swimming Pool on a blazing sunny day in the summer of '78.

My mate knew a group of girls, so we ended up sitting with them.

Michelle was part of the group, and as soon as I laid eyes on her, it was game on.

The problem was … I was painfully shy.

So the only tactic I could think of to attract Michelle was to act the fool, make her laugh.

It sort of worked.

But when it was time to leave, I couldn't find the courage to ask her out.

And there she was, gone.

Disappearing into the sunset like the closing scene of a film I hadn't been brave enough to star in.

All night, I regretted my lack of courage.

Even the agony of Mum treating my sunburn with Epsom salts couldn't distract me from the missed opportunity.

The next day, ignoring the blistering heat and the fresh sting of yesterday's sunburn, I decided to take a chance, and returned to the pool, solo, on a quest for Michelle.

Lady Luck was on my side.

Michelle was there, with her friends.

I spent the day acting the fool again, and as Michelle and her friends were leaving, I popped the question:

Me: "Hey Michelle, can I take you to the cinema next Friday?"

Did she fall at my feet?

Nope.

Michelle: "Uhm … not sure."

Then one of her friends intervened, and accepted the date on her behalf.

That was the first warning sign I ignored.

For the rest of the week, I floated on air.

Even Mum's second round of Epsom salt treatment couldn't wipe the smile off my face.

I still bear the scars of love.

Two swimming pool visits left me with severe sunburn, and freckle-like spots on my biceps and shoulders.

Ah … the things we do for love.

It's Friday night outside the cinema.

I'm standing there on my own, wondering if Michelle will stand me up.

Then, suddenly, from around the corner, she appeared.

My heart started racing …

then instantly slowed again, as her friend appeared …

then another …

and another …

until all the girls I'd met at the pool surrounded me.

Turning this date into a romantic evening was going to be a challenge.

Sharing my pack of Jelly Tots with Michelle proved difficult, she was at one end of the row of seats … I was at the other, separated by six friends.

Halfway through the film, her friend next to me, clearly tired of watching me nibble sweets solo, leaned forward.

Michelle's Friend: "Michelle, you should be sat here."

Michelle reluctantly swapped seats.

Still determined to impress, I offered her some Jelly Tots.

She instantly refused, so I knew the arm-over-the-shoulder routine was a no-go.

Sitting there, picking Jelly Tots from between my teeth, I began plotting how to convince Michelle I was the boy of her dreams.

At the end of the film, I tested our fragile relationship.

Me: "Michelle, can I walk you home?"

Michelle: "Uhm … not sure."

Again, her friend intervened, and accepted my proposal on her behalf.

We walked home alone and in silence.

All the way, I was working up the courage to attempt handholding.

Curiosity won.

I reached out … and bingo, we were holding hands.

Just as we reached her house.

Michelle: "This is where I live," she said, trying to vanish through the front door with the speed of a hunted gazelle.

To this day, I believe she meant to go in alone, but in her panic, she forgot we were still connected by digits.

I found myself standing in the hallway. With Michelle.

Now this is where it got really, really weird. And I mean *weird*.

A door opened, and there, standing in front of us, was Sylvia.

A close friend of our family.

A woman I'd known forever.

Sylvia: "Hello! Who have we got here?"

I gripped Michelle's hand like it was a parachute cord.

The Floating Frog

In my head:

Me *(internal monologue)*: "Sylvia! Who the hell do you think it is? It's me, Steve Rowley! I don't understand this game … you're freaking me out!"

Michelle: "Hi Mum, this is Stuart."

What?

She got my bloody name wrong.

Me: "No, it's Steve."

Michelle: "Oh yes! That's right."

She got my name wrong.

She got the wrong mum.

And her wrong mum was pretending not to know me.

Had aliens invaded Earth while we were in the cinema?

Did they press the reset button in Sylvia's head?

Sylvia: "Nice to have met you."

Then she disappeared through a doorway.

Michelle was practically on her knees, begging me to release her hand from my death grip.

Me: "Sorry, I got nervous meeting your mum."

Blood began returning to her white knuckles.

Using her good hand, she opened the front door and started pushing me.

Moments later, we were outside, face to face, for the goodbye scene.

Still undeterred, I homed in for a goodnight kiss.

To my amazement … she didn't move.

Our lips engaged.

Thanks to Zoe, I knew the full power of my kissing technique.

So, after snogging Michelle for a short while, I became concerned, she hadn't turned into a Dyson vacuum cleaner.

Curious about what was happening on her side of the kiss, I sneaked a peek.

I opened my left eye … only to find her right eye staring directly at me, from very, very close quarters.

"Arghhh!" we screamed in unison, then jumped backwards in a state of shock.

At that moment, any thoughts I'd had about a career in optometry vanished.

We stood there in silence.

Both utterly embarrassed.

Still, not one to give up easily.

Me: "Can I see you tomorrow?"

Michelle: "I don't think so."

I was shocked.

Not as shocked as the pupil-to-pupil stare-down moments earlier, but still … pretty shocked.

So, was this the end of Michelle and me?

I needed to know.

Me: "Is that your final answer? Or would you like to phone a friend?"

The door slammed shut in my face.

It really did feel like:

As one door closes … another one slams in your face.

Interlude:

The Wrong Mother Situation – Explained

I found out a while later that Sylvia has an identical twin.

And I mean identical.

Same voice.

Same body shape.

Same hairstyle.

Even more bizarrely, Sylvia's son was the mate who introduced me to Michelle.

Which makes Michelle … his cousin.

So, no keeping this tale secret.

Side Note:

The conjoined twins are also identical, but much easier to identify.

Colin is on the left.

Brian on the right.

Outerlude:

Where was I? …

The Vanishing Vacuum

So, it was time to play my next shot.

I got my trusty wood out again … and swung.

This time, the ball landed at the feet of Sharon, standing right on the edge of the green.

By the time I got to Sharon …

I was sixteen years old.

The Freemans Cigar Factory break-up Christmas parties were legendary, and not for the faint-hearted.

Held at a local club near the factory, they featured loud music, drink, food, and my favourite:

GIRLS!

This was my chance to find the girl of my dreams, or at least someone to enjoy the party atmosphere with.

I was not disappointed.

Sharon, a stripper I occasionally chatted with during her shift, made a beeline for me as I walked in.

Just to clarify:

Girls who removed stalks from tobacco leaves in the cigar factory worked in the stripping room and were known as "strippers".

The Sharon I knew up until that point was easy-going, fun to chat with, a nice, young-ish girl from the Welsh Valleys.

I'm not sure what happens to Valley girls after a drink or two … but I was about to find out.

After a quick "Hi", Sharon grabbed my hand and dragged me onto the dance floor.

The music was pumping, and I prepared to impress everyone with my dance moves.

Yeah, my dance moves?

I'm one of those people who, if you mute the sound, could be up there with the best of them.

Unfortunately, with the sound on … it's painfully obvious I can't move to the beat.

I personally think it's a unique talent to be naturally half a beat out from the rest of the world.

So, if you're ever at a concert clapping to the rhythm and hear a phantom echo … turn around and give me a wave.

I was already dancing to *Stayin' Alive* by the Bee Gees before we even hit the floor.

So, in the zone, I felt like I should've been wearing a warning sign:

"Hot to touch."

When we reached the dance floor, I pirouetted and launched into my full John Travolta routine.

I playfully beckoned Sharon to join me.

As she came closer, I heard a familiar noise …

Before I could place it, the Dyson Deluxe vacuum cleaner called Sharon had engaged for a full-on snog.

I'll be honest, I was not expecting that.

Genuinely shocked.

So there we were, locked in a passionate snog, on a packed dance floor.

As I closed my eyes, I pictured us on an exotic beach … a bit like Barry Island.

Lush.

Sharon was in full vac mode.

I'd officially entered the world of tonsil tennis, with tongues.

Being a polite young man, I returned serve.

It went on for ages, and I didn't want it to end.

Especially once I realised I could do something

I never knew I could do … breathe through my ears.

I was in utopia.

No need to check Sharon's side of the kiss this time.

Then, real magic happened.

Like a seagull squawking over a dropped chip, I heard someone yell across the dance floor:

"Shazza! Your Cinzano Bianco's on the bar!"

Then, poof!

Sharon vanished like a magician's assistant.

There I stood, middle of the dance floor.

Eyes closed.

Head tilted.

Tongue extended … in a vain attempt to reunite with Sharon's, or should I say Shazza's, tonsils.

After a few failed tongue probes, reality kicked in.

I was immediately transported from the golden sands of Barry Island … back to Planet Dance Floor.

I slowly opened my eyes.

And Sharon was gone.

Then, walking towards me like an irate sergeant major, came my sister, who also worked at the cigar factory.

Irate Sister: "Put your tongue back in your head, idiot, and get off the dance floor. You're a total embarrassment."

As she turned away, she added, just loud enough to land the final blow:

Irate Sister: "Next time, wear baggy trousers. Everyone can see how much you enjoyed that dance."

One prick, and the love bubble I'd been sharing with Sharon had popped.

I was now the centre of unwanted attention, praying someone would buy me a Cinzano Bianco … so I too could go "poof!" and disappear.

Long before Michael Jackson became a werewolf, I had already performed the moonwalk.

Want to check my claim to fame?

- **Location:** Currans Club, Cardiff

- **Date:** Christmas 1979

- **Time:** Just as Shazza was knocking back her fifth Cinzano Bianco

To avoid the obvious walk of shame through the crowded bar, I made a tactical retreat to the fire escape behind me.

Head held high, with a shit-eating grin stretched across my face to hide the excruciating embarrassment … I invented the moonwalk.

Everyone thought I was striding forward with confidence, but here's the clever bit:

I was actually gliding backwards towards the fire exit.

Once I reached my destination, I pirouetted, pushed open the doors, and escaped, fire alarms ringing in protest.

The moonwalk was born.

Outside, it was time for my next shot.

On the Job Job

I rested my wood, then walked onto the green with my putter in hand.

By the time I got to the ball, I was seventeen.

I wasn't quite sure how to play my final stroke, luckily, I was joined by an experienced caddy: twenty-two-year-old Gertrude.

OK, obviously not her real name.

I need to protect myself from lawsuits. Plus … she had a big brother.

Gert had the body that belonged to a model, and the face that didn't.

That's the lawyers sorted. Now it's just her brother to worry about.

I met Gert at the petrol station where my mate worked.

No instant attraction, but one afternoon I got into a friendly tussle with Gert after she took my car keys.

We ended up face to face, her hands behind her back, clutching the keys.

Mine holding hers, trying to retrieve them.

There was that awkward pause … where I wasn't sure whether she wanted me to steal a kiss, or headbutt me.

We'll never know.

The guy from Pump 3 was getting impatient, so she let go of the keys and returned to the counter.

The next time we were alone was at her house.

I'd left the cigar factory, now a second-year apprentice electrician.

And quite possibly, it was my wrestling skills that landed me the job, rewiring Gert's house.

So, let's finish the game of golf.

I was upstairs in the bathroom, making a hole in the ceiling for the shower pull switch, when Gert walked in.

Gert: "Why have you made that hole up there?"

A cheeky smirk curled across my face.

Me: "So I can spy on you when you're having a bath."

As I climbed into the loft to install the cable, Gert shouted.

Gert: "I'm having a bath. So, no peeking."

Then she shut the bathroom door behind her.

Me *(whispering)*: "But I'm still installing the cable …"

I was being paid by the hour, so I felt obliged to continue.

Did I have a sneaky peek at the beauty of her body, foam-filled and swishing around?

Absolutely not, Gert's brother. Never. Not once. Not even a peek.

With the bathroom wiring complete, I moved on to installing cables under the floorboards in Gert's bedroom.

She wandered in, scantily dressed in loose clothing.

Gert: "Do you like being an electrician?"

Me: "It has its benefits …"

Now, this is the part where the caddy removes the flag from the flag home, and you carefully line up your final shot.

Gert: "Can you do this?"

She did a headstand against the bedroom wall.

From that point on, I don't think I spoke another word.

Gravity played its part, her top dropped, revealing her assets.

And I must say … they were genuinely nice assets.

Oh my God.

I turned my head to act like a gentleman, but my eyes refused to follow instructions.

They were locked onto nature's beauty.

Or rather, beauties.

Gert returned to her feet.

Gravity re-established.

She walked over, grabbed my hand, and led me to her bed.

I carefully lined up my shot.

Gert encouraged me to take my time.

I gripped my shaft tightly, then, with an enthusiastic stroke … my shot was on its way.

Halfway through, I suddenly thought of protection.

Gulp!

The only protection I had was a pair of safety boots, which, in this particular situation, were bloody useless.

The game came to a sudden climax as my shot landed in the flag home.

I had successfully completed a round of golf at the Cherry Top Golf Course.

Moments later, I shook hands with Gert like a gentleman golfer, she lay on the bed, cigarette poised.

Then, without a word, I went straight back to pulling cables.

What else was I supposed to do?

I didn't smoke.

Gert, unimpressed by my swift departure to the clubhouse, and annoyed I didn't linger for the celebratory cigarette on the green, decided she could no longer be my caddy.

As I left the Cherry Top Golf Club,

I was farewelled with a cheerful:

"Thank you for coming."

And awarded a golden lottery ticket for the monthly Worry Draw.

The comedian Mickey Flanagan has his "Out Out" catchphrase.

I, on the other hand, have my own:

"On the Job Job."

Although I don't think I'll be touring any time soon.

Filthy Films

The Hidden Secret

To an eleven-year-old boy, the female anatomy was best explained by the schoolyard rhyme:

"Milk, milk, lemonade … round the corner, chocolates made."

And the really rude bit? That was a fu fu or a penny slot, depending on which cousin you asked.

One afternoon, while playing hide-and-seek with my younger cousins, Jack and Carl, I decided my aunty and uncle's bedroom would make a great hiding spot.

As I scanned the room, something caught my eye, a glossy magazine on the bedside table.

On the front cover: a beautiful woman with no clothes on, strategically covering her milk, milk, lemonade with her arms and hands.

That looks interesting, I thought.

I tilted the magazine towards me.

Playboy.

Just as I was about to turn the page, one of my cousins burst through the door.

Cousin: "Ha! Caught you!"

I closed the page quickly.

Me: "No, I didn't look."

Cousin *(confused)*: "What?"

Then I realised, they meant caught me in hide-and-seek.

Me: "Yes! I, uh … I meant I didn't look, for a very good hiding place. Yes, that's what I meant."

What a recovery.

You don't have to teach male instinct, it just kicks in.

Curiosity had got the better of me. I told my cousins it was my turn to seek, but this time it was for the Hide-and-Seek World Championship, which meant they had to hide in the best place possible: the garden.

To give them a fair chance, I said I'd count to a thousand before commencing Operation Seek!

Me: "One, two, three, four …"

In a flash, they disappeared through the bedroom door.

I moved to the bathroom and peeked through the window, watching them scatter across the garden lawn.

Me *(louder)*: "Twenty-three, twenty-four, twenty-five …"

Everyone else in the house was downstairs chatting, so I seized my moment and crept back into the Playboy bedroom.

I stood in front of the magazine, flipping through the pages, searching for the woman from the cover.

A few pages in, there she was. Dressed as a maid. Well, almost.

Her top was clearly not up to the job, unable to contain her beautiful milk milks. I stared, wide-eyed.

WOW! What a discovery.

Hugh Hefner certainly knew how to wean boys off *The Beano* comic.

With nervous excitement, I turned the page. And there it was, the chocolate-made moment.

She was facing away from the camera, feather-dusting a polar bear who, judging by his expression, had just returned from a taxidermist appointment.

Her outfit had clearly lost the battle, her knickers had slipped to her ankles, revealing a perfectly shaped bum.

Somewhere in the middle of all this, I felt a strange but oddly enjoyable sensation, similar to the one I'd experienced sliding down the floor-to-ceiling rope in primary school.

Suddenly, I remembered my cousins.

I rushed back to the bathroom.

Me *(loudly)*: "One hundred and ninety-eight, one hundred and ninety-nine, two hundred …"

Back in the Playboy bedroom, I returned to my new *Beano* comic.

I flipped back to the chocolate maid page, same pocket sensation, now with the addition of a twitch in my left eye.

I took a deep breath and turned the next page …

Holy Mother of God, the lemonade page.

I was not ready for that.

The maid, now entirely without knickers, was perched on a chair, one foot on the floor, the other casually flung over the armrest like she was airing out her laundry.

It was bold. It was baffling. It was … a full-frontal education.

Even the polar bear wore a stunned expression.

What followed was a jaw-dropping revelation: hairy, unexpected, and utterly baffling to an eleven-year-old boy.

I spun the magazine around, trying to make sense of what I was looking at, like one of those magic-eye puzzles that never quite came into focus.

Between this and the recent heartbreak of learning that Father Christmas only existed in shopping centres, my world was officially upside down.

I ran back to the bathroom.

Me: "Four hundred and ninety-nine, five hundred …"

Then back again to the Playboy bedroom, questioning whether I really wanted to cancel my *Beano* comic subscription.

Maybe the maid image wasn't that confusing?

I turned back to the lemonade page.

Yep. It was confusing. (It would take me a few more years before I was able to solve the puzzle.)

Then a loud voice called out from downstairs:

Dad: "Steve, time to go!"

I quickly closed the Playboy magazine and put the tissue box back on top.

As I passed the bathroom window, I shouted,

Me *(even louder)*: "Six hundred and ninety-nine, seven hundred …"

I left my uncle and aunty's house that day a little bit wiser, and a lot more confused.

Oh yes, my cousins.

They did actually become Hide-and-Seek Champions of the World.

And if they're ever found, they'll be presented with their well-deserved medals:

Nine hundred and ninety-nine … one thousand.

And me?

I never looked at polar bears the same way again.

Sword Swallowing for Beginners

Graduating from Playboy magazines to adult VHS films happened when I was an apprentice electrician.

Another electrician and I, Andy, a good-looking guy and well aware of it, were installing electrical storage heaters in a flat in Cardiff.

Andy's eyes lit up when he spotted a VHS tape tucked beneath the coffee table in the lounge.

He picked it up and turned to me, holding out the case with its handwritten film title scrawled across the cover.

Andy: "Do you know what this is?"

Me: "Uhm … *Deep Throat*? Is it a teach-yourself sword-swallowing video?"

Andy: "Dickhead."

Me: "Is that a clue?"

We both giggled childishly at the find.

Just then, Sue, the lady of the house, walked in.

Sue: "What are you guys laughing at?"

She spotted the tape in Andy's hand.

Sue: "Oh my God! That's my boyfriend's, not mine. Honestly!"

This was Andy's cue to activate full-on cheeky-chappie mode.

He started flirting, teasing her about the tape's ownership.

Sue was lapping up the attention.

Meanwhile, like a true professional, I continued installing the storage heaters, leaving them to enjoy their schoolyard romance.

Just as the giggling reached maximum volume, it stopped abruptly.

Andy suddenly appeared by my side.

Andy: "Sue and I have had a chat and decided it's time for you to watch your first-ever adult film."

And since an apprentice must always obey the electrician's command, I entered the lounge, sat down in the armchair, pulled out my cheese-and-pickle sandwiches from my lunchbox, placed the lunchbox on my lap, and awaited the matinee.

There were no opening credits.

No build-up.

The tape had clearly been left where the last viewer had stopped, mid-action.

My eyes opened wider than wide, and my half-eaten sandwich fell out of my mouth onto my lap.

What was I watching?

This was definitely not a magic-eye puzzle.

The answer was right there, staring me in the face, as it was for the actress on the other side of the TV screen.

And it had very little to do with sword swallowing, though the theme felt oddly familiar: a troubling disregard for gag reflexes.

Within seconds, I was unable to stand without giving the game away, the film was clearly having an effect on me.

Embarrassment swiftly overtook excitement.

I tried to look away.

My eyes refused. Traitors.

Concentrating furiously, I managed to convince my eyes to cooperate and began counting the leaves on a plant next to the TV, an attempt to reduce blood circulation and distract the growing betrayal happening north of my lunchbox.

A challenging task, as I suffer, like most humans, from that pesky thing called peripheral vision.

And as the main source of entertainment for Andy and Sue, I was desperate to escape this humiliating scene.

I quickly picked up my half-empty lunchbox in a vain attempt to hide my own personal full lunchbox. I made a dash for the hallway, leaving a trail as the remains of my chewed-up cheese-and-pickle sandwich fell to the floor.

My hastily Groucho Marx–inspired walk was accompanied by hysterical laughter before Andy and Sue resumed more intense flirting.

The situation between them made me feel uncomfortable.

I began to feel like a spare part on an adult film shoot, unsure where to put myself.

I was installing a cable inside a walk-in wardrobe when Andy reappeared.

Andy: "This is your lucky day, mate. Not only have you watched your first porno movie, but you also get to have the rest of the day off. Pack your tools up and disappear."

From the wardrobe, I produced a pair of Ronald McDonald–sized climbing boots and a lumber jacket that would've hung loosely even on Arnold Schwarzenegger.

Me: "I think you might have a bit of trouble if her boyfriend comes home."

Andy: "He's got to catch me first! Bye-bye, off you go."

And once again, like an obedient apprentice, I left.

I have no further evidence of what shenanigans took place in the flat once I had left … Your Honour!

The rest of my day was spent calculating my finances, plotting how to buy my own VHS player.

Not for educational purposes, obviously.

Just … curiosity.

Play, Pause, Panic

So, staying with the VHS player theme …

In the mid-80s, video shops were everywhere.

The novelty of choosing your own movie, not relying on terrestrial TV, was liberating.

The only downfall was the dreaded *On Hire* sticker.

You'd spend forever choosing your film, only to find that some bastard had got to it first.

My local video shop, Video Video, was owned by Ray, a friendly guy, always game for a quick chat.

I was in there one time with my girlfriend.

Having chosen a film, we went to the counter.

Ray: "How's things, Steve?"

Me: "Yeah! Good, mate."

Then Ray shrugged his shoulders like a market street trader and glanced left, then right, then behind us.

It wasn't a big shop, so it was obvious, just the three of us.

Ray: "You guys interested in a blue one?"

Me: "Uh?"

Ray: "You know, a sex film. A 'porno'."

Me: "OH …"

I looked at my girlfriend, who wasn't looking impressed.

Me: "Has it got a good storyline?"

To this day, I still can't believe I asked that question.

Ray disappeared below the counter, then reappeared enthusiastically.

Ray: "Here's one, *Rings of Passion*. This one's got a storyline."

I looked to my girlfriend for approval.

She didn't say no, so I took that as a yes.

Me *(enthusiastically)*: "Let's go for it."

The tape went into a discreet blank case, and off we went.

As luck would have it, my parents had taken my nan to Portsmouth to visit my uncle for the weekend.

Lucky for us, because they had a VHS player, and we didn't. We'd just started renovating our house.

A bottle of Lambrusco, accompanied by a large packet of Jelly Tots.

We were ready to be entertained.

Just for you film critics out there,

The storyline was…

The husband has a quick "how's your father" with his secretary and presents her with a ring for her good work.

The secretary then shags somebody else and passes on the ring.

The shagging and ring relay continues, until the wife ends up with the ring.

The husband returns from a hard day at the office, shags his wife, and spots the ring on the bedside cabinet, shocked, to say the least.

The end.

Now, here's the best part about VHS tapes, rewinding the film while it's still in play mode.

Basically, watching the whole thing backwards… at speed.

What was meant to be a "turn-you-on" movie instantly transformed into a rib-tickling comedy.

The funniest part?

Watching the male actors clean up their mess with handheld vacuum cleaners.

I walked my girlfriend home, then returned to the scene of the crime and went to bed.

On Sunday morning, I woke up ready for a few hours' work at the house we were renovating with my builder friend, Archie.

I grabbed my car keys, and, more importantly, the video case, as Mum and Dad were on their way home.

I swear my mum went to the same school as Mother Teresa, which meant I'd need more than a prayer mat if she found the *Rings* film.

With the discreet video case tucked into the glovebox, I went to Archie's to pick him up.

After a few hours of graft, it was tools down and off to the pub for a couple of well-earned pints.

My turn to get the drinks. I placed them on the table and sat down for a natter.

Archie: "What are your plans for the rest of the day?"

Not wanting to discuss my newly acquired fetish for watching adult films in rewind.

Me: "Mum and Dad are back from their break, so I'll spend a few hours with them."

Then I double-checked in my head that I'd definitely put the video case in the glove compartment.

I definitely put it there, 100%.

I took a slurp of my pint.

Then I had a thought so terrifying I choked and spat a mouthful of lager all over Archie.

Archie: "What the fuck!"

Me: "Sorry, mate! Sorry, it's an emergency. I'll be back in a bit!"

I ran to my car and yanked open the glovebox.

I pulled out the video case and slowly opened it,

Empty!

I'd forgotten to take the VHS tape out of the player.

Shite! Shite! Shite!

I jumped in the car and raced to Mum and Dad's, praying I'd get there first.

Nope. Their car was already parked outside.

Fuck! Fuck! Fuck!

I gingerly entered the house in full SAS mode.

I opened the lounge door slowly…

There was Nan, sat alone in front of the TV, watching…

You guessed it.

Sunday Worship.

Phew!

Me: "Hi Nan, how was your holiday?"

Nan: "Lovely, thank you. How was your weekend?"

Me: "Good, thanks."

I swiftly moved to the VHS player and hit eject, reuniting the tape with the empty case.

For those unfamiliar with old VHS eject mechanisms,

they sounded like a drawer of cutlery being emptied onto a tiled floor.

The noise summoned Mum, out of nowhere.

Mum: "Hello! What are you doing?"

Me: "I forgot to take a film we hired out of the player. Need to get it back to the shop, pronto."

By then, Rings of Passion was safely tucked away in its blank case.

Mission accomplished. Stress levels: downgraded from Defcon 1 to mild palpitations.

Time to change the subject.

Me: "How was your holiday, Mum?"

Mum: "Hang on! What was the film?"

Oh my God! Why the questions?

Me: "Just a boring action movie, you know, villains beating each other up. Kings of Bashing."

Mum: "Oh my God, that was your rude film!"

Me: "No! What are you talking about?"

I replied, wearing my brightest red, innocent face.

Mum: "I'll tell you what! When we came home, I sat Nan in front of the TV, turned it on, then went upstairs to unpack…"

Me: "Oh shit."

Mum: "Twenty minutes, Steven. Nan watched that filthy film for twenty minutes. Disgusting!

I was blaming that new Channel 5 station!"

Me: "Why didn't Nan turn it off?"

There was a pregnant pause as Mum considered her reply.

Mum: "I don't know. I think she was enjoying it."

Nan *(chuckling)*: "Oh yes!"

That sent me into uncontrollable hysterics.

Mum: "Don't you EVER bring filth like that into this house again."

Me: "Nan, do you want to watch it in rewind?"

Nan *(grinning)*: "Yes please."

Mum: "No, no, no! Get out, and take that 'FILTHY FILM' with you!"

Back at the pub, I returned to my seat.

Archie: "What the hell happened? You looked like you'd seen a ghost."

Then he took the final mouthful of his lager.

Me: "My mum accidentally put a porno film on TV for my nan to watch."

Archie choked, then returned serve, spraying me with the last of his pint.

I relayed the entire episode.

Archie: "I didn't see that one coming.

Bet your nan did though."

To this day, every time I see Archie,

he greets me with:

"Seen any good films lately?"

Steve Rowley

Football Tackle

Unwanted Consistency

When it comes to football, I was always destined to become an electrician.

I was never going to be scouted by the likes of Leeds United, my favourite team.

My first club was Sea View Under 8s.

We had three teams: the A team, the B team… and I, naturally, played for the C team.

I always thought A stood for attitude.

The boys in the A team were incredibly good players, and they knew it.

They'd never hesitate to let everyone else know it, too.

Basically, I was jealous of the talented bastards, and not afraid to admit it.

That said, all my best mates played for the C team. And we had one thing in common:

We were crap at football, and everybody knew it. Even the goalposts looked embarrassed.

We turned up every week for each other, regardless of the weather or the looming humiliation.

Our goal net caught more balls than the number of fish Captain Birdseye caught in his fishing net. And that man had a bloody boat.

I don't remember our team winning a single game in the three seasons I played.

But we were consistent.

Painfully so.

At eleven years old, I retired from football and turned my attention to playing a different field, chasing romance instead of goals.

Six seasons later, still no wins.

Turns out, consistency wasn't just a team trait. It was personal.

Bedknobs and Slapsticks

Fifteen years after hanging up my boots, I made my return to the soccer field.

At twenty-six, I was the elder statesman of the team, older, wiser, and slightly more prone to hamstring injuries.

A couple of old mates had convinced me to join their team. They were desperate.

And if you're desperate, I'm your man.

Some of the players had just come up from the youth league and were thrilled to have a few mature bodies alongside them.

Over the next few seasons, we developed into a formidable football side.

We reached the dizzy heights of third from bottom in the local lower league.

Our manager was so impressed with our development, he organised a tour to play Ilfracombe Town Football Club in North Devon.

Our accommodation was a sprawling Edwardian boarding house.

The entrance sat at ground level, housing a large TV room and a couple of guest rooms at the front.

The basement served as reception and restaurant.

Then came the Stairway to Heaven, leading to countless guest rooms on the upper levels.

I couldn't tell you how many floors there were, but given the complimentary oxygen masks and altitude sickness tablets at reception, I suspected quite a few.

An ideal training ground for climbers prepping for Everest.

Thankfully, Pete and I were allocated a twin room on the first level, above the entrance.

Management's safety policy seemed to follow an age-based floor plan:

Elders at the bottom, teenagers at the summit.

The room was basic:

Two single beds so close together, if Pete had a bad dream, I could reach over and hold his hand without getting out of mine.

The "en suite" was accessed via a paisley-patterned curtain.

Inside: a sink and toilet, both tastefully stained with the rich history of previous tenants.

After I'd settled in, I popped down to reception to use the payphone and let Em know I'd arrived safe and sound.

On the way back to my room, I was confronted by a bullish-looking guy standing in the hallway, blocking my path and staring me down.

I glanced behind, just to check I wasn't caught between him and his arch-enemy.

Nope. Just me and him.

There was no way past, he filled the corridor like a brick wall with a pulse.

It felt like I was about to start the Gauntlet Run on *Gladiators*.

I took a deep breath and offered my best Wallace & Gromit cheesy grin, the kind that usually screams harmless and slightly terrified.

He didn't even blink.

Just as the imaginary *Gladiators* referee roared, "Contestant ready!", a real voice called out from the guest room behind him.

Mystery Voice: "Robbie, what are you doing out there? Come on, Robbie, be a good boy and come back into the lovely room.

You can have some cake."

With that, Robbie turned and vanished into the room like a rehomed rhino.

As I passed the room, a woman was gently guiding Robbie to a chair beside a table with a cake on it.

It was only then I realised, poor Robbie was mentally challenged.

I returned to my room, still feeling a little guilty about my first impression of Robbie.

He wasn't a Gladiator.

He just wanted cake.

It was a relief to leave the boarding house and hit the town before our friendly match against Ilfracombe Town the next day.

And when I say "friendly", I don't mean friendly-friendly.

Just an unofficial contest, no medals, no mercy.

The word "friendly" in football… is like calling a military invasion a scenic detour.

The whole team met up for a slap-up meal at the local McDonald's.

To me, it felt more like a slap-down than slap-up.

Yep, it's an age thing.

I finished my banana thickshake and McFlurry ice cream, then it was time to go nightclubbing at the disco.

After a few pints, I was starting to feel my age.

I did fancy showing off my dance moves, but that would've meant dancing with a female, which, to me, felt like being unfaithful to Em, my brand-new girlfriend.

I mentioned my predicament to one of the younger guys, and he promptly volunteered his services.

Youthful Teammate: "No probs, Steve. I'll dance with you."

Upon hearing this, I instantly choked on the pint I was slurping, spraying atomised lager droplets into the air.

I'm old school, no woman, no dance.

Me: "Dance with another guy? Are you kidding?"

Youthful Teammate: "You won't dance with us, but you're not worried about having a shower with the team after a match?"

He looked genuinely perplexed.

Ah, the innocence of youth.

Then I glanced at the dance floor, and realised half our football team were dancing with each other.

Including Pete.

Swaying enthusiastically with our goalkeeper.

Not a chick in sight.

I decided to make my exit before the slow dances kicked in, and the lads started smooching together.

There's only so much I can take.

And Pete slow-dancing with our goalkeeper was dangerously close to my limit.

I told Pete I was heading back early, via the fish and chip shop for some proper food, then back to base camp: our one-star accommodation.

Pete fancied a few more drinks, and a couple more dances with our goalkeeper, so he decided to stay.

But Frostie, one of the youngest on the team, overheard the words *fish and chips* and eagerly volunteered to join me.

So we left the nightclub and headed to the local greasy restaurant.

I ordered pie and chips, and Frostie ordered his.

We ate them as we wandered back to our accommodation along the main road.

For reasons only Frostie knows, he suddenly jumped up and slapped an old display sign hanging above the doorway of a boarded-up shop.

The cracked Perspex shattered onto the pavement below.

At ten at night, the noise was amplified beyond belief, it genuinely sounded like a ram raid.

Me: "You bloody idiot! What are you doing?"

Frostie: "Shit! I didn't expect it to fall out, I was just seeing if I could reach it."

A mature couple walking behind us froze at the sound, then spun around and retreated in the opposite direction.

Me: "For Christ's sake, Frostie, put your hands in your pockets until we get back to the hotel."

Just as we reached the boarding house, Starsky and Hutch pulled up beside us in their police car.

I spun to Frostie and whispered aggressively,

Me: "Keep your mouth shut. Let me do the talking."

Then I turned to Starsky, or maybe Hutch.

Starsky or Hutch: "Evening, lads. We've had reports that two guys walking up the high street smashed a shop window."

Me: "Really? We've just walked up the street, we didn't see anything. There were a couple of lads messing about, but I didn't see them do anything."

By now, my nose had grown longer than my moral compass.

Starsky or Hutch: "So, what've you guys been up to?"

Me: "We've got a football match against Ilfracombe Town tomorrow. Just popped into town for a quiet pint and some fish and chips. Now heading back for some shut-eye."

I pointed to our boarding house.

Starsky glanced at Hutch.

Hutch glanced at Starsky.

I could tell they weren't entirely convinced.

Starsky or Hutch: "OK, fellas, enjoy the rest of your evening."

Me: "Thank you, officers."

They drove off slowly… turned around… and cruised past again.

I gave a friendly wave while muttering under my breath,

Me *(quietly)***:** "Frostie, you are a dickhead."

Back at the boarding house, we headed to the TV room.

Me: "Frostie, I'm watching telly, I'm still rattled from our police cameo."

Frostie: "Yeah, I'm wide awake too, I'll join you."

Ten minutes into some action film, I heard the door creak open behind me.

Frostie had a full view of the TV room visitor.

His face said it all.

Frostie *(trembling)***:** "There's a naked guy at the door."

I spun around, Robbie. Stark naked. No slippers. No shame.

Me: "Don't worry, he's harmless. That's Robbie. I met him earlier… when he had clothes on."

As if summoned back to another dimension, Robbie vanished.

Frostie *(panicking)***:** "Where's he gone?!

Where's he gone?!"

I checked the corridor, nothing.

Guest room doors: closed.

Robbie Houdini'd.

As I turned, Frostie was so close to me I briefly considered phoning Em to confess I'd been unfaithful.

Frostie: "Where the hell did he go?"

Frostie's teeth were chattering like castanets.

Frostie: "That's it – I'm off to my room!"

Two strides later, he vanished up the stairs. Bedroom-bound.

I finished the film and headed to bed.

Thirty minutes later, I was jolted awake by what sounded like a full-on sword fight – just outside the entrance.

My first thought: the team had brought trouble back with them to the boarding house.

I rushed down to the locked front door. By the time I got there, everything had gone quiet.

Not sure what to expect, I opened the door slowly – foot braced against the bottom, ready to repel any enemy forces on the other side.

Instead, I was greeted by a disgruntled Pete, standing in the entrance conservatory.

Me: "What the hell happened to you?"

Pete: "You! You bastard!"

Me: "Me? How come?"

Pete: "You buggered off early and took our only hotel keys. I couldn't get in, so I lay down on this bloody sunbed."

He pointed to a sad-looking frame – no cushions, just springs.

His right leg was still tangled in it, like a reluctant hostage to bad furniture.

Pete: "I was waiting for one of the other guys to show up and let me in."

Me: "So what was all that noise?"

Pete: "When I turned over, I fell through the frickin' springs, the sunbed collapsed, and I had to fight my way out."

I tried to look concerned.

But I snorted – and burst into hysterics.

Pete: "Fuck off."

I opened the door to let him through.

Pete didn't move.

He just stared straight past me, mouth agape.

Pete: "Who the hell is that?"

I knew that look.

I turned – Robbie.

Still naked.

Still slipperless.

Me: "That's Robbie. And before you ask – I have not had sexual relations with that man."

While Pete shook loose from the sunbed like a man escaping a bear trap, Robbie pulled off his signature move: the legendary vanishing act. No puff of smoke. Just gone.

Back in our room, totally exhausted, I hit the pillow and drifted instantly into dreamland.

Peace at last.

Thirty minutes later, I was jolted awake again, this time by knocking at the door.

Really?

Was this night never going to end?

I opened the door – and three of the team came crashing in, pushing past me and making a beeline for the beds.

Me:"What the hell are you guys doing?"

Drunk Team Member: "We can't get into our room. Frostie's shoved furniture up against the door and won't answer."

Frostie had barricaded himself in – thanks to the roaming Robbie.

By the time I closed the door, two players had already collapsed on my bed, while the goalkeeper curled up in full spoon with Pete – who remained blissfully unaware.

Pete *(murmuring in his sleep)*: "Hand ball, Ref!"

With the beds fully occupied, I fell asleep for the third time.

This time, in an armchair.

Like a king who'd surrendered – no throne, no dignity, just upholstery and defeat.

In the middle of the night, I was jolted awake yet again by a sharp pain in my gut.

A couple of sneaky farts later, the pain was still there.

Please, no.

I'd officially entered the food poisoning regurgitation phase.

The pie I'd eaten a few hours earlier had decided – just like Robbie – to make a dramatic reappearance.

I locked myself behind the paisley curtain of the bathroom and quietly emptied my system from both ends.

Easier said than done: the sink was too far from the toilet to multitask.

Add a lack of toilet paper and the looming threat of someone wandering into my war zone – this was not one of my finer hours.

Like any nuclear disaster, the clean-up operation remains classified.

Eventually, morning arrived.

With a flushed-out system and questionable dignity, I woke up feeling… hungry.

I took a very overdue shower, then headed to the restaurant for a cooked breakfast with the team.

As I walked in, everyone cheered. Word on the pitch was, apparently, I had a new boyfriend.

'Rob the Knob.'

Bastards.

Even my supposedly best mate Pete couldn't help himself – he joined in.

Laughter filled the room at my expense.

Then, right on cue, the laughter stopped.

Smiles dropped.

Horror spread across their faces.

Yep.

Robbie had appeared in the restaurant doorway behind me – still in his birthday suit.

But this time… wearing slippers.

Now it was my turn to return fire.

Me: "Boys! That's not the only tackle you'll have to deal with today!"

With that, Robbie yet again performed his legendary vanishing act.

And the most amazing fact about this tale?

We beat Ilfracombe Town, 1–0.

No tactics.

No sleep.

Just pie, panic, and a naked man in slippers.

Football, eh?

Bloody beautiful.

Steve Rowley

A Proper Love Story

Two Pints of Lager and a Wife Please

So, let's set the scene.

The year: 1991.

The date: August 2.

This translates to 2/8/1991… or, if you're from Planet Trump: 8/2/1991.

Also – to make this the ultimate romantic tale – we'll completely ignore that it's my ex-fiancée's birthday.

'Twas a beautiful summer evening, so what better way to spend a Friday evening than at the Cwm Ciddy – an Olde World pub on the outskirts of town?

It was the place to meet for a few drinks before moving on to nightclubbing at the disco.

My mate Adrian and I elbowed our way through the packed lounge, eventually arriving at the bar.

Task one: complete.

The next challenge? Attracting the attention of one of the bar staff and ordering drinks.

Interlude:

I know I'm not the only one – but I somehow manage to become instantly invisible the moment I touch a pub bar.

People walk in, sit down, order food and drinks, have dessert, enjoy their meal, pay the bill, and leave – all while I'm still standing there, waving a tenner like a UN peacekeeper in a war zone.

I'm considering starting an 'Invisible Bar Person Support Group' on Facebook.

Outerlude:

Where was I?…

Eventually, I managed to get the attention of a bar person.

Me: "Two pints of lager and a packet of crisps, please."

As I picked up my pint, I turned towards Adrian, who by then had his back to me – chatting up a girl.

I tapped him on the shoulder.

Me: "Adrian, your drink is on the bar."

Adrian: "Cheers."

Then he turned to grab his pint.

As he moved away, I found myself gazing into the eyes of the beautiful creature he'd been chatting to.

My first words to my future wife were:

Me: "So what are you doing for the rest of your life?"

Beautiful Creature: "Marrying you."

It was like a full-blown love scene from a Hollywood movie.

Something epic. Something timeless. Something… like Shrek.

I had found my Fiona.

And from this point on, she will be known as Em.

By the time Adrian turned back around, Em and I had already started choosing names for our children.

She favoured Samuel or Oliver.

Unfortunately, I had to spoil it – my two dogs were Sam and Ollie.

Em wasn't too keen on my alternative suggestion: 1 and 2.

Anyway, Adrian wisely clocked the situation and stepped away from the love vortex.

Adrian: "I can see I'm not wanted here."

Then wandered off into the crowd.

Our love was cast in stone – for eternity.

Well… almost.

Bronze Medal Breakups and Gold Medal Lies

There were just a few loose ends to tie up before our relationship could fully flourish.

Namely: the two girls from work I was seeing at the time.

Now, before you all start tutting – I was in between relationships.

What do I mean by that?

Let's look at it like a 'Relay Race'.

The first leg was complete – my ex-fiancée had handed the baton to Girlfriend 1.

My relationship with Girlfriend 1 was more or less over.

All that remained was the ceremonial bronze medal presentation for successfully completing her leg of the race.

Then came Girlfriend 2.

She was mid-leg when I met Em.

This was trickier.

Luckily, Em helped me draft the script for my resignation phone call.

It started well. I explained to Girlfriend 2 that I wasn't in the right headspace for a relationship due to the recent break-up with my ex-fiancée.

What a storyteller.

Everything was going smoothly, exactly as rehearsed.

Then came the curveball I hadn't planned for:

Girlfriend 2: "But I'm willing to wait… for as long as it takes."

Crikey!

The script had no contingency plan.

Panicking, I considered declaring I was entering the priesthood – but we worked in the same building.

So, I had no choice but to disqualify Girlfriend 2… for accidentally stepping into somebody else's lane, rejecting any requests for a stewards' enquiry.

After meeting Em, the relay race was officially complete.

I'd crossed the finish line.

A Gothic Experience

A couple of weeks later, our relationship was to be tested.

I was at a nightclub with Adrian when he decided to show off his dance moves to a girl he'd been chatting to.

So, he left me holding our drinks.

Just as I was sneakily topping up my pint with Adrian's, a Gothic chick appeared out of nowhere.

She stared for a moment, then spoke:

Goth Chick *(matter of fact)*: "Oh! Do you want to dance or what?"

I glanced at the two pints.

Me: "With or without the drinks?"

She immediately took both drinks, placed them on a nearby table, grabbed my arm, and dragged me onto the dance floor.

Soon, she leaned in:

Goth Chick: "Are you a contractor or what?"

Now that's one I hadn't heard before.

Me *(curiously)*: "Why's that?"

Goth Chick: "Because I only fuck contractors."

Bloody hell, I thought – no way I was missing this opportunity.

Me *(comedy mode)*: "God damn it! No, I'm not a contractor... I'm actually a full-time lollipop man."

That reply... did not go down well.

She stared at me in disbelief.

Goth Chick: "Fuck you!"

"Are you fucking gay or what?"

Then she disappeared from the dance floor in a cloud of rage and imaginary smoke trails.

I was very disappointed, mainly because I didn't even get the chance to get my lollipop out – and safely guide her through the busy dance floor traffic.

Adrian was still mid-flirtation, so I left early.

Jumped in a taxi – ten miles in the opposite direction… to Em's house.

I got there just before midnight and started throwing stones at her bedroom window.

Eventually, blurry-eyed Em appeared.

Em: "Oh my God, Steve! What are you doing here?"

Me *(slightly slurring)*: "I've just moved in next door and was wondering if you could spare a cup of sugar?"

One minute later, I was in the hallway.

As I tried to tell her about my Gothic experience, she kept whispering:

Em: "Shhh! – you're going to wake everyone up in the house!"

Too late.

Em's dad appeared at the top of the stairs.

Em's Dad: "What's going on?"

Em: "Uhm… Steve… Uhm…"

I stepped in.

Me: "Michael! It's all good – go back to bed."

Michael – formerly known as Em's dad – gave a wry smile.

Michael: "Oh! OK. I've been told."

Then he vanished back into his bedroom.

From the moment I met Em's dad, it was clear we'd never have a typical father-in-law/son-in-law relationship.

We were destined to be besties.

If anyone else had spoken to Mike – formerly known as Michael – like that, he'd have marched them straight out… and fed them to a nearby pack of Gothic chicks.

As for Em's mum…

From day one, it was clear we'd have a textbook mother-in-law/son-in-law relationship.

Having successfully avoided Mike feeding me to a pack of Gothic chicks, the following morning my dad came to retrieve me from Em's house.

On the way home, I asked Dad to swing by the Spar supermarket for cereal and milk.

So, with a box of cereal in one hand and a carton of milk in the other, I stood behind a guy buying his morning paper at the checkout.

He paid and moved on – leaving me face-to-face with the checkout chick.

Or should I say… the Gothic checkout chick.

We both did a double take.

Then silence.

She wore a name badge, so now I had a name: Nessa.

Last night, Nessa had plenty to say.

Now? She couldn't even look at me.

I activated my pub bar invisibility mode – thankfully, no need for the UN peacekeeper flag.

She took the items from my hands.

Last time she took two items off me, things escalated.

I held my breath; half expecting her to grab my arm and drag me to the meat and veg aisle.

As she scanned them, I stared at the notice board behind her.

One ad caught my eye:

"Electrical contractor needed. Apply within."

I paid and left – no words exchanged.

She'd gone one step further than the night before.

This time, she'd managed to serve me.

Call it irony.

Call it fate.

A month later, I was made redundant.

And guess what my next job was?

Yep.

An electrical contractor on a chemical plant.

Somewhere, Nessa was probably still scanning cereal boxes…

Still refusing to serve lollipop men.

The One Franc Engagement

A year into our relationship, Em and I booked a romantic weekend in Paris.

We stayed in a small hotel near Notre Dame – everything was perfect.

The only issue for me? Breakfast.

Where the hell was my full English? All I could get was croissants, jam, and extra strong coffee.

Bloody foreigners.

The first time Em was genuinely disappointed with me happened at the top of the Eiffel Tower.

The scene was set – we were in one of the most romantic places on earth.

All that was required was for me to go down on one knee and propose to the love of my life.

No way was that going to happen.

For someone with a fear of heights, this was one of the most unromantic places on earth.

I was trying my hardest to look cool and sophisticated – while facing the threat of losing control of bodily functions at any moment.

Definitely not a one-knee moment.

That moment had to wait another 24 hours.

After recovering from my journey to the top of the giant French Meccano construction, next on the list was…

The Louvre Museum.

Paradise for the arty-farty – but not for a boy from Barry.

After queuing for 30 minutes, we finally stood in front of the Mona Lisa. I must admit, I was disappointed. I didn't quite get the vibe.

It was like looking at someone constipated, sitting behind a double-glazed window. Then again… maybe she wasn't constipated.

Maybe she was just French.

Wow! – look at me. I'm turning into an art critic.

Personally, I would've extended my stay in the Louvre if the Mona Lisa had been replaced with the iconic 70s Athena Tennis Girl poster.

The poor lass, playing tennis, who'd obviously, in her rush to get to centre court, forgotten to wear knickers.

A nasty paparazzo caught her checking for her spare tennis ball… under her skirt… revealing her bum.

The bloody cheek!

That evening, we headed to the Moulin Rouge area of Paris.

The Floating Frog

It was almost dusk, so the place to be was the steps of the Sacré-Cœur – a stunning white Catholic church overlooking Paris – perfect for watching the Eiffel Tower lights turn on.

Em and I sat snuggled up, watching as the lights lit up the tower.

A quick snog.

We climbed the remaining steps and entered the Sacré-Cœur.

It was breathtaking inside – absolutely stunning.

Then the moment happened.

Wandering down the aisle, I turned to Em and dropped to one knee.

She instinctively tried to help me up before reality kicked in.

Me *(oozing romance)*: "Em. Will you marry me?"

It took a while for Em to speak.

With tears in her eyes,

Em *(tearfully)*: "Yes."

Then continued to cry.

I understand her first reaction – I didn't produce a ring.

There's a simple reason: I didn't have one.

It's all about timing. And the time was right – with or without a ring.

After another snog, all loved up, we headed for the hustle and bustle outside the Moulin Rouge.

Across the road from the windmill, we spotted a tacky gift shop, still open.

In the side window – a selection of plastic and metal rings.

Perfect!

Em chose her engagement ring from the jewellery box.

Genuine tin, with an intricate lattice pattern – clearly sculpted by a ten-year-old in a Chinese sweatshop with a loose grasp of symmetry.

I felt on top of the world, so money was no object – I handed over one franc (pre-euro) to the shopkeeper – like a man investing in romance.

Mission accomplished.

We returned from Paris, and Em's dad, Mike, picked us up from the airport.

Just as we pulled up outside our house, I did the traditional thing – asked his permission to marry Em.

I think he got more emotional than Em did during the proposal.

Eventually, Mike said, "Yes."

And just like that, the one-franc engagement was officially endorsed.

Marriage for the Over Twelves

After telling friends and family, the response was always:

"Congratulations! When's the wedding?"

Our dishonest reply:

"We haven't made any plans yet – probably in a couple of years."

The truth? We had made plans.

We were going to elope to Gretna Green for a secret romantic wedding.

Interlude:

Now, for those unfamiliar with Gretna Green – a brief history lesson:

England, 1754 (that's the year, not the time):

Anyone under 21 needed parental permission to marry.

Technically, you could marry without it, but the clergyman who performed the ceremony would spend 14 years behind bars.

Meanwhile… in Scotland…

The laws were different – still technically British, but a lot more relaxed.

Minimum marriage age: boys 14, girls 12.

As long as the couple weren't related, a blacksmith could legally marry you.

Gretna Green is a small Scottish town, just over the English border, and became the go-to spot for rebellious, pimply-faced English teens.

They'd pop over, get married in the forge, and be home for supper.

Mum: "Hello love. How was school today?"

Spotty Teen: "Great. Got married."

"What's for tea?"

The ceremony was simple:

Blacksmith: "Are you of marriageable age?"

Spotty Teens: "Yes."

Blacksmith: "Are you free to marry?"

Spotty Teens: "Yes."

Blacksmith: "Have you washed behind your ears today?"

Spotty Teens: "Yes."

Clang! Strike of the anvil.

Blacksmith: "You're now married." Barbie and Ken signed the witness papers.

Tiny Tears caught the bouquet.

Marriage: sealed.

Some writer chick called Jane Austen later helped turn these rebellious weddings into romantic fairytales.

Outerlude:

Where was I?..

Romance Versus Mishaps

The only box we were unable to tick was having our wedding day on Valentine's Day.

It fell on a Sunday, and the Gretna Green registry office was closed.

Having told the family we were off to Chester for a short holiday, we secretly set off for Scotland in my 1974 Alfa Romeo GTV classic sports car.

Inside, it had that wonderful old-car aroma. The boot, however, smelt like a tramp's shoe.

To counter the stench, everything packed in the boot was tightly sealed in plastic – including Em's wedding dress.

First port of call: the local petrol station.

With a full tank of fuel, it was non-stop to Gretna Green.

Well… not quite.

Just as we left the station, I remembered I hadn't checked the air pressure in the spare wheel.

Too late to turn around, so I headed for the next petrol station.

We pulled up at the air section, and I quickly jumped out – just as it started to rain.

Em sat in the front seat, buzzing for the big day.

Meanwhile, I opened the boot.

Me *(panicking)*: "Em! Em! Get out here – quickly!"

By the time she got to the back of the car, her wedding dress was on top of the roof, and the rest of the boot contents were scattered across the forecourt.

Em: "Oh no! Steve, what's happening?"

Did Em think I was having second thoughts and wanted her relay baton back?

Not a chance.

The smell of tramp's shoe had been replaced by a new fragrance:

'PETROL DE FUMES'.

Me: "The fuel tank has split."

The bottom of the boot was awash with petrol.

Me: "We have to get everything inside the car."

Em: "But there's not enough room."

Me: "It's going in."

Just then, a guy watching the chaos unfold while fuelling his car strolled past towards the kiosk.

Forecourt Comedian: "Strange place to have a car boot sale."

Ignoring him, I set about the task of cramming everything outside the car… inside – including Em.

It was like one of those ridiculous challenges from Top Gear.

Mission complete, I collapsed back into the driver's seat.

Em was no longer in the passenger seat – she had been replaced by suitcases and boxes of shoes.

She'd been relocated to the back seat, buried somewhere beneath luggage and the hangie-up clothes.

A frantic couple of hours later, we were back en route to Gretna Green.

The Alfa Romeo was in a mechanic's workshop. And we were now travelling in Em's not-so-romantic Austin Maestro.

Six hours later, we finally arrived at the Chinese Garden Hotel in Gretna Green.

Totally exhausted, we checked into our separate rooms.

We'd booked them to stick to the tradition of not seeing the bride or her dress before the wedding.

Unless Em planned to wear a black dustbin liner down the aisle, I still hadn't seen the dress.

After settling in, we went to the restaurant together for our final meal as single people.

I'm still not quite sure how a Chinese Garden fits into the Gretna Green wedding theme… but it did make a brilliant backdrop for the photos.

I was mildly disappointed to discover that chicken fried rice and prawn crackers weren't on the menu.

Instead, I had to settle for some posh dish I'd never even heard of.

I'm a Barry boy – I don't do posh.

But I did know not to mop my plate with bread at the end of the meal.

Interlude:

When I say I don't do posh, I mean I'm not programmed for it.

I was once in the upper-class Howells department store in Cardiff when I felt the urge for a pee.

I asked a shop assistant where the men's toilets were.

Shop Assistant *(poshly)*: "The men's cloakroom is behind you, sir."

I didn't ask where to leave my coat – I thought the poor old dear hadn't heard me correctly.

Me: "Sorry, I need the men's t-o-i-l-e-t, toilet."

Shop Assistant: "Yes sir, the men's c-l-o-a-k-r-o-o-m, cloakroom is behind you."

What was this about?

In school, a cloakroom is where you hang your coat before class – and boys' toilets are where you play who can pee up the wall the highest.

Outerlude:

Where was I?…

The Wrong Man

Meal finished, Em and I had a final snog as single people before disappearing into our separate rooms.

The next time I would see Em was at the altar.

So, there I stood, waiting for the love of my life to walk down the aisle behind me.

Well… Em didn't initially walk down the aisle. She froze as soon as she saw the back of me standing at the altar.

Em *(totally confused)*: "That's not him. That's the wrong man."

Unbeknown to Em, I'd swapped our carefully chosen wedding suit for a full Scottish Highlander outfit – Prince of Wales tartan kilt, sporran, the works.

All I was missing was the Billy Connolly accent.

I had to turn around before Em would continue down the aisle towards the man in the skirt.

My princess arrived at my side, looking totally stunning.

Em couldn't resist.

Em *(concerned)*: "I hope you're wearing something underneath your kilt?"

All of this was captured on video by our cameraman witness. The other witness? The photographer.

With the ceremony complete (without further incident), we were whisked off to the blacksmith's forge for our second wedding.

Em was definitely over 12 – and she was definitely not my sister.

The resident blacksmith married us again, sealing it with a strike of the anvil.

So, if Em ever has enough of me… she'll have to divorce me twice.

That means she gets half of everything in the first divorce – then half of my half in the second.

Best I behave.

We returned to the Chinese Garden Hotel for photos and yet another posh meal.

Then it was time to pack Em's Austin Maestro and begin our two-hour journey to our honeymoon destination: Johnstounburn House Hotel, just outside Edinburgh.

The journey turned out to be quite interesting.

At every opportunity, we popped into local shops – searching for ice lollies to soothe my rapidly worsening sore throat.

Scottish summer temperatures are freezing.

In winter – they're borderline Antarctic.

So, asking a Scottish shopkeeper for an ice lolly in February drew some remarkable responses.

Scottish Shopkeeper: "We dunny even sell ice lollies in the summer, you eejit."

I had to settle for packets of throat lozenges and cold cans of lemonade.

Desperate measures for desperate throats.

By the time we arrived at Johnstounburn House Hotel, the throat lozenges had done their work – normal service resumed.

We wrapped up warm and went for a romantic walk around the grounds of the seventeenth-century hotel, entertained by ducks attempting to land on a frozen pond.

The perfect evening included a candlelit dinner with champagne, followed by a wee dram of Scottish whisky as a nightcap. Then it was off to our room, which had a four-poster bed.

No separate rooms on our honeymoon night.

After revealing what a Welshman wears under his kilt, we fell asleep in a warm embrace.

Married life looked perfect.

Not sure how Em felt when she woke at 4 a.m. to see me sitting on a chair in the corner of the room – wearing a shower cap and waving at her.

Had she found out too late that her brand-new husband had a fetish for synchronised swimming?

All I needed was a peg on my nose and it would've been grounds for instant divorce.

Em *(confused and concerned)*: "Oh my God, Steve! What are you doing?"

Me: "It's okay – I still have that tickly throat." (Spits out a throat lozenge.)

I'd been up for the last hour, quietly gargling in the bathroom.

Then I spotted the complimentary shower cap and decided to wear it in a vain attempt to distract Em from the sword fight raging at the back of my throat when she woke up.

Luckily, there were no complimentary pegs.

I managed a few hours' sleep after my synchronised swimming routine.

By the time I woke, the lozenges had worked their magic – our day out in Edinburgh was back on.

After breakfast, we jumped in the Austin Maestro and set off for the 30-minute drive into the city.

As we searched for a car park, the sword fight resumed – this time with reinforcements. My temperature had decided to join the battle.

It wasn't long before I had to concede defeat.

Me: "Sorry Em, I'll have to pull over – you'll have to drive. My head's spinning and I don't feel safe driving."

Em: "I'm getting you to a doctor."

As hard as we tried, no doctor's appointment was available.

Em *(teacher mode)*: "That's it. We're going home. You need antibiotics."

There were no negotiations. It was an unconditional surrender.

We packed our bags, climbed into the car, and hit the road.

All I remember from the 8-hour drive was watching motorway signs counting down the miles to the next town… then desperately trying not to swallow until we reached each exit.

Only then would I allow myself to gulp the saliva – now textured like broken glass.

Back home, we parked the car a few streets away so family wouldn't know we were back. This gave me time to recover – and us time to plan our big reveal.

In the meantime, Em phoned for a doctor.

One hour later, I was perched on the edge of the bed with a very enthusiastic young female doctor bouncing behind me, placing her stethoscope all over my back.

Em and I exchanged raised-eyebrow glances as the doctor wrapped up her trampoline routine.

Doctor: "You've got very nasty tonsillitis. Here are some antibiotics."

And off bounced Doctor Tigger to her next appointment.

The Elopement Games – No Flowers Required

I slept for eight glorious hours without the need for a shower cap.

I probably could've slept for 24 – but Em woke me with a look of shock.

Em: "Your mum's on the phone… and she knows we're home!"

Me: "What the hell?"

I picked up the phone.

Me: "Hi Mum."

Mum: "Hi love. Why are you home so early?"

Me: "Bit of a sore throat. How did you know we were home?"

Mum: "I have your wallet."

How? What? Where? When?

The same wallet I'd used in Scotland to buy throat lozenges the day before… now in my mum's possession.

Me: "I don't understand?"

Mum: "Mark from across the road dropped it off this morning. His mate found it on the pavement near your house, saw the address on your licence, 'which you haven't updated', and gave it to Mark last night."

The wallet must've fallen out of my pocket while parking stealthily.

Me: "Wow… lucky. I'll pick it up later."

Now the pressure was on.

With tonsillitis under control, my genius shifted into high gear.

The plan: invite family over under false pretences. Em would don her wedding dress and wait in the front room. I'd film their reactions.

Time to put it in motion.

Contestant One: Em's sister.

She'd been living with us and had no clue.

As she walked in –

Em's Sister: "Oh wow – your wedding dress! You look beautiful. When's the big day?"

Em *(displays her ring)***:** "We were married on Tuesday."

Em's Sister: "I can't believe you kept this secret! I'm a trained police officer – how did I miss it?"

Contestant Two: Em's dad, Mike.

Excuse: We'd told him Em was feeling poorly and needed his spare video player.

As he walked in and spotted Em – he dropped the recorder.

Mike: "You bastards. You bloody bastards. This is fantastic!"

Contestant Three: My mum and dad.

Excuse: I needed my wallet.

They were overjoyed. Eventually, Mum grew a bit teary.

Mum: "I wanted to be there."

Contestant Four: My sister and family.

Cue: hugs and kisses.

Final contestant: The mother-in-law.

Her reaction? Less joy, more silent fury.

She couldn't forgive the secret elopement – or the fact that she'd missed her daughter's big moment.

Her protest was both elegant and enduring: twelve months of complete silence. No contact. Not a word.

Ever since, I've unsuccessfully suggested to Em that we secretly renew our vows yearly.

And to finish our love story…

On our wedding day, Em actually said:

"Steve, you have been so romantic – you never have to buy me flowers again."

Does Em regret saying that?

Let's just say the florist industry doesn't know my name.

Parenting

Renovation, Reproduction, and Rottweilers

Em and I quickly settled into our carefree married lifestyle.

Short holiday breaks.

Long holiday breaks.

Meals out. Drinks out.

And numerous romantic nights in.

Life was perfect.

Why would we want it to change?

A couple of months after the wedding, we bought our first house together.

It was a "fixer-upper", which is estate agent code for bring a sledgehammer and a roll of wallpaper.

But we were excited.

This was going to be our family dream home.

With the contract signed, the estate agent handed us the keys.

We headed straight there.

I unlocked the front door, turned around, picked Em up in my arms, kissed her, and carried her over the threshold.

Romantic perfection.

Well… it only lasted about five seconds.

The lovely old lady who sold us the house had lived with lots and lots of cats.

And, with the best of intentions, she'd decided to shampoo every piece of mouldy old carpet before leaving.

As soon as we stepped into the hallway, all hell broke loose.

It felt like we'd been ambushed by someone wielding pepper spray.

The aroma of cat piss was so overpowering, I nearly dropped Em.

We staggered back out into the front garden, coughing and retching.

Ten minutes later, still without the ability to speak, we looked at each other and nodded.

Operation 'Carpet Extraction' began.

Within the hour, every piece of mouldy, cat-piss-soaked carpet was piled in the front garden.

That was the start of our house renovations.

By the end of the first week, we'd magically transformed the main upstairs room into a temporary bedroom/living room/kitchen combo.

Luckily, there was a separate toilet – so we had at least one room with dignity.

It was an adventure.

And we were loving it.

Every spare moment was spent working on the house.

Well… almost every moment.

The Ovulation Overlord

The only thing more important than the renovation was the medieval ritual of the ovulation cycle.

Yes – we were also trying for children.

Sharing my life with someone as beautiful and caring as Em was a dream come true.

I felt blessed.

What I wasn't expecting was the other woman who possessed Em's body during ovulation.

I became a sex slave – I felt like a bottle of Martini – any time, any place, anywhere.

Within two months, the sex fiend who occasionally possessed Em vanished.

Em used a positive pregnancy test stick as a wand to perform the exorcism.

When Em surprised me with the news, we made a decision.

Since our house still resembled a one-bedroom building site, Em and her bump would move back in with her dad until the renovations were complete.

That left me and my two dogs – Sam and Ollie – to fend for ourselves.

At one stage, the back door had been temporarily replaced with a curtain, so security was… let's just say, non-existent.

Luckily, I had backup.

Sam – a Rottweiler cross Great Dane – was strong, agile, and terrifying to anyone who didn't know he was a big softie.

The Midnight Mauling

One night, I was in a deep sleep when I was suddenly pinned to the bed by a heavy weight on top of me.

Everything was pitch black.

My arms were trapped under the quilt. I couldn't move.

Knowing that the ovulation sex fiend had left the building site, I instinctively called for Sam to come to my rescue.

He didn't come bounding in.

He didn't need to – he was already on top of me.

It took thirty seconds and a lot of sloppy licks to the face before I broke free from the attention-seeking mutt.

Thank God ovulation wasn't part of the equation.

Sam was a true protector.

It would take someone brave – or very stupid – to break into our house.

But if I introduced someone to him?

They were instantly a friend for life.

They could break in, pin me down, lick my face – and Sam would just sit by the bed, patiently waiting for his turn.

Six months later, Em and her rotund belly moved back into our newly renovated home.

A month after that, Elliot was born at 2:50 pm.

That's ten to kick-off in the world of football.

I was due to play in a football competition.

But no – Elliot clearly had no respect for fixture lists and decided to arrive three weeks early, just to ruin my last ever game of competitive soccer.

Twenty months later, the final member of the future Welsh three-man toboggan team arrived: Megan.

She decided to be born on Leap Year Day.

One birthday every four years?

Result!

No, no – that's not how Megan operates.

She celebrates her birthday on February 28 every year.

And every four years?

She has a double birthday – February 28 and 29.

By then, I'd been demoted to number six in the Rowley household – just behind the dogs and the washing machine.

I settled into parenting.

Joule the Ghoul and the Letterbox War

One of my main challenges was keeping the kids entertained when Em managed to get time off for good behaviour.

One afternoon, while Em was out shopping, I decided face painting would be a fantastic way to keep a 4 and 6-year-old occupied.

Using my artistic flair, I transformed Megan into a cat and Elliot into a lion.

Pleased with the results, I couldn't wait for Em to walk in and shower me with praise for entertaining the kids without the aid of a TV remote.

Unfortunately, she wasn't due home for another hour.

So, to keep the kids occupied a little longer, I let them face-paint me as an elephant.

What a great dad, I thought.

With both Megan and Elliot gently applying brushstrokes of grey and black across my face, I began to drift off to the soothing rhythm of their concentrated breathing.

Heaven!

Suddenly, I was jolted awake by a loud knock at the front door.

It took a few seconds to come to my senses.

The kids were now sat in front of the TV, watching *Asterix and the Vikings*.

Me *(shocked)*: "Who's at the front door?"

Megan *(without turning)*: "Dunno, Dad."

Why did I ask?

How were they supposed to know?

I jumped up and headed for the front door.

On the way, I passed by the toilet. The door was open, and I caught a glimpse of something in the mirror – staring at me.

I stopped dead.

What had I just seen?

I took a few steps back and stared back into the mirror.

Jumbo the Elephant had become Joule the Ghoul – a creature straight out of Michael Jackson's *Thriller* video.

What had the kids done to me?

Another knock.

Too embarrassed to open the door, I went into "old man with a runny nose" mode.

Me *(shouting)*: "Who is it?"

Knocker: "I'm here to save you money!"

Me: "What? Have you kidnapped my wife?"

Knocker *(slightly agitated)*: "No! Can you open the door and I'll explain."

Me: "I'm not allowed to open the door to strangers."

Knocker: "I can save you loads of money – just by switching electricity suppliers. I just need your signature."

Me: "No thanks. We haven't got electricity. Everything this side of the door runs on coal and candlelight."

Knocker: "Well, I'm posting the forms anyway."

Me: "No, you're not."

Knocker: "Yes, I am."

And so began the letterbox war.

He tried to post the forms.

I held down the flap from the inside.

Me: "How's your end going?"

Knocker *(very agitated)*: "Fuck you!" With that, he stomped off, muttering expletives.

Victory was mine!

I clenched my fist, power-pumped the air, and spun around.

Me *(whispering)*: "Who's the daddy?"

Only to find the cat and the lion standing behind me, watching their father display the diplomacy skills of a five-year-old.

Somewhat embarrassed, I handed the TV remote to Elliot and spent the next thirty minutes scrubbing Joule the Ghoul off my face… before the next challenger knocked.

The Welsh Three-Man Toboggan Team

Another tale from that era takes us to a snowy afternoon walk – with the dogs and kids in tow.

I had the dogs on leads in one hand, and with the other, I was dragging the kids behind me as they sat on a little plastic toboggan.

Then came the bright idea.

I tied the toboggan rope to Sam's collar.

Success.

Sam instantly transformed into a Husky dog.

With Ollie on one side of me and Sam on the other, the setup was perfect.

Sam pulled the kids behind him like a seasoned sled dog.

What could possibly go wrong?

As we turned into our street, heading down the slope towards our house, the toboggan decided to go full Winter Olympics.

Woosh!

The toboggan, now travelling faster than Sam, slammed into his back legs – knocking them forward.

And there they were:

• Elliot at the back

• Megan in the middle

• And at the front, sat upright and proud – Team Captain – Sam.

The Welsh Three-Man Toboggan Team.

They flew past me, screams of excitement echoing down the street.

I couldn't pull Sam's lead – it would've turned the toboggan sideways and caused utter carnage.

All I could do was let go and attempt a snow sprint, trying to grab Elliot's shoulders to slow them down.

Not a chance.

I'd entered full Mr Bean mode – arms and legs flailing, slipping and sliding like a giraffe on roller skates.

Poor Ollie was like a canine yo-yo, being yanked in every direction by his out-of-control owner.

By some miracle, the toboggan glided into our driveway and gently came to rest on the grass outside the front door.

I arrived, flustered and breathless, still in full panic mode.

Sam casually stepped off, strolled to the nearest bush, and created a bit of yellow snow.

Welsh Toboggan Team: "That was brilliant, Dad! Can we do it again?"

AGGGH!!

The Fast and the Fetal

It was another six years before the ovulating sex fiend returned – resulting in Number 3: Alfie.

Alfie was a car fanatic even before he was born.

He tried to make his entrance into the world while we were still in Em's Ford Escort, en route to the maternity ward.

He almost succeeded.

The final stretch of our hospital dash was through rush hour traffic.

We were bumper to bumper on a narrow country road.

Em was desperately trying to hold onto Alfie when I spotted the hospital entrance – 200 metres away across farmland.

The only things in our way?

A field and a couple of hedges.

I did contemplate making a dash across the field on foot.

But then I looked at Em.

She was in no fit state to emulate Red Rum in the Grand National.

Eventually, we arrived at the maternity ward car park.

Alfie's arrival was imminent.

In full panic mode, I parked in the only available space:

A disabled bay.

Em: "You can't park here. I'm not getting out."

She point-blank refused to open the door.

Off we went in search of a non-disabled bay.

Meanwhile, Alfie was staging one final attempt to enter the world – in the footwell of the car.

Em sensed his determination.

Em: "I can't hold on! Get back to that bloody disabled park! NOW!"

Three minutes after walking through the maternity ward doors, Alfie entered the world at 100 mph.

The midwife didn't deliver him – she caught him.

The Rowley family was complete.

Parenting Highlights Unleashed

Some may say my parenting skills are questionable.

But the results speak for themselves:

• Elliot is a qualified electrical engineer.

• Megan, using her leap year status, is technically only 7 years old – and already the youngest police sergeant ever.

• Alfie is a professional radio presenter and classic car expert.

Parenting Highlight 1: Child of the Week

One of my proudest innovations was the introduction of "Child of the Week" in the Rowley household.

Not necessarily awarded to the best-behaved child.

For example:

• Completing homework = 1 point

• Successfully getting away with not completing homework = 3 points

For reasons I still don't fully understand, Em – an ex-schoolteacher – strongly disagreed with my methods.

Parenting Highlight 2: King of the Forecourt

Ever since he first watched Disney's *The Love Bug*, Alfie's obsession with Herbie – and every other VW Beetle – had been borderline religious.

So, you can imagine his reaction at age 8, when the garage door opened to reveal a 1963 VW Beetle.

Then I told him:

Me: "This is your Herbie."

He didn't just smile. He levitated.

These were the days when VW Beetles were still affordable.

Alfie already had an exceptional knowledge of classic cars and loved nothing more than chatting to other classic car owners about their pride and joy.

Though, once, he had to put one in their place.

The Petrol Station Showdown

We were out for a cruise in Herbie and pulled into a petrol station.

As I got out to fill the tank, a guy checking the pumps shouted over:

Obnoxious Pump Checker: "Oh look! A turtle on roller skates!"

I ignored him and kept filling.

Alfie jumped out and followed me into the kiosk.

The same guy was now behind the counter.

Obnoxious Pump Checker: "How long have you had the turtle?"

Me: "It's my son's Beetle. It's his pride and joy."

I hoped that would soften him.

Nope.

Obnoxious Pump Checker: "Your son's car? What did he do wrong to deserve that?"

Clearly, a closet comedian.

Me: "Alfie's a Herbie fanatic. A classic car fanatic. I don't think there's a car on the road he doesn't know."

The obnoxious pump checker decided to put Alfie to the test.

Obnoxious Pump Checker: "Is that right? I've got a 1970 Ford Mustang Mach 1. Know what that looks like?"

I looked at Alfie, waiting for him to fire back with some obscure Mustang facts.

Alfie: "Yes."

The guy gave me that look – 'Sure he does.'

He obviously thought we were flower-loving hippies with no clue.

Obnoxious Pump Checker *(killer blow mode)*: "Okay, smart guy. My favourite classic car is the Bel Air '57. Know that one?"

Alfie: "Yes."

Now I was sweating.

This was no time for 8-year-old Alfie to go into 8-year-old mode.

The guy was ready to chalk us up as clueless.

I was about to wave the white flag and retreat to our roller-skating turtle.

Then – just as I turned to leave – the cavalry arrived.

The Mic Drop

Alfie: "The Chevy Bel Air '57 – that was the final year of the Tri-series. The '55, '56, and '57 were Chevy's most popular American cars of the '50s."

BOOM!

The obnoxious pump checker blinked.

Victory was ours.

Alfie wasn't showing off.

He was genuinely interested in the guy's choice of cars.

He had no idea the man was being derogatory about Herbie – he just wanted to talk shop.

Meanwhile, I was moonwalking towards the exit, basking in the glory of Alfie's petrolhead mic drop.

I even considered grabbing a family pack of crisps from the shelf, opening it, and launching the contents into the air to create my own ticker-tape parade.

Behind me, the obnoxious pump checker's jaw hit the counter with a thud – schooled by an innocent eight-year-old.

Parenting Highlight 3: No Ambulance Required

3 am. Elliot appears at the foot of our bed.

Elliot: "Mum, Dad, I've got terrible stomach pains. Something's not right."

I assessed the situation with my usual medical precision.

Me: "Go sit on the toilet. You just need a good old poo. Night."

He toddled off. I went back to sleep.

The following morning, up early. Off to work I go.

2 pm. Phone rings.

Em: "You need to get to the hospital ASAP. Elliot has appendicitis. He needs emergency surgery. You absolute TWAT!"

Parenting Highlight 4: X-Rated X-Rays

During soccer training, I kicked a ball towards Megan.

She caught it – but then immediately dropped it as if it was a hot coal.

"Dad, that really hurt my wrist."

I examined it.

Me: "Doesn't look swollen. Can you move your fingers?"

Megan grimaced as she slowly wiggled her fingers.

Me: "There you are, nothing broken. Try five press-ups."

Megan, holding back tears, completed them.

Me: "Just a bit of bruising. You'll be fine in a couple of hours."

She finished the football session.

The following morning, up early. Off to work I go.

2 pm. Phone rings.

Em: "Megan is in a cast. Her wrist is broken. You absolute TWAT!"

Interlude:

This wasn't my first brush with X-ray vision failure.

Our friend Linda once came home from horse riding with a disfigured wrist.

I diagnosed it as a dislocation.

I held her hand in one hand, her arm in the other.

I was just about to yank her hand quickly to reset her wrist when I paused and thought:

"Maybe best to let a qualified medical professional handle this."

Linda returned from hospital with a TV mast sticking out of her arm – her wrist shattered and pinned with miniature scaffolding.

The thought of Doctor Rowley's un-dislocating procedure is not for the squeamish.

Outerlude:

Where was I?…

Oh yes… parenting.

Parenting Highlight 5: The Ant and the Ice Cream

One day, while watching Megan play football, Alfie came running over – bawling his eyes out, snot and tears everywhere.

Alfie: "Mummy, I've been bitten by an ant and it really, really hurts!"

Me: "For Christ's sake, Alfie. Stop screaming. You're embarrassing us."

Alfie *(crying, stuttering)*: "Bu-but D-Dad, it really hurts!"

Me *(unsympathetic)*: "Stop crying."

Another football mum chimed in:

Football Mum: "You've never been bitten by a black ant, have you, Steve?"

Me: "No."

Football Mum: "I have. It bloody hurts."

Softy mums, I thought.

A few weeks later, I took Alfie to the Noosa Classic Car Hillclimb.

While walking towards the top section, I tripped over a piece of wood – wearing open shoes.

Pain shot through my toe. I looked down.

A piece of dark wood was sticking out of it.

I bent down and pulled it out –

Suddenly it grew six legs.

In my shock, I dropped the bloodthirsty black ant – losing any chance at vengeance.

Then the pain hit top gear. Unable to unclench my jaw, I hopped around in agony, condemning the unrepentant sinner to hell.

I hadn't felt pain like that since Leeds United lost the 1973 FA Cup Final.

At one point, I considered amputation as my only option.

Meanwhile, Alfie was stuck on repeat:

Alfie *(needle stuck)*: "Dad, was that an ant?"

Thirty seconds later:

Alfie *(needle stuck)*: "Dad, was that an ant?"

Eventually…

Me: "YES! But don't tell your mum."

"If you don't tell her, I'll buy you an ice cream."

I hobbled back to the car park, bought Alfie an ice cream, and headed home.

Em: "How was your day?"

Me: "Really good. Alfie loved it."

Em: "Did you like all the cars, Alfie?"

Alfie: "Yes."

Em: "Which one was your favourite?"

Alfie: "A Porsche 356. But I didn't see it race because Dad got bitten by an ant, and he was in so much agony we had to come home early."

Me: "ALFIE!"

Alfie: "Sorry, Dad. I forgot I wasn't supposed to tell Mum about the ant."

Em: "You absolute TWAT!"

Needless to say, Alfie was not Child of the Week.

Alfie was 8 years old at the time of the black ant saga.

Eleven years later, he became the official commentator for the Noosa Classic Car Hillclimb.

When it comes to parenting, I am – without question – a compulsive 'absolute TWAT'. And I wouldn't change a thing.

Steve Rowley

Parading

Bad Memories

Christmas Day 2025.

I was sitting at the dinner table with my family, playing a trivia card game called Do You Really Know Your Family? – the kind of wholesome chaos specifically designed to expose everyone's deepest secrets before pudding.

My turn.

I drew a card.

The question: "What is your most embarrassing moment?"

I had to think of the answer silently while the family guessed which humiliation held the top spot.

Whoever guessed correctly would win the card – and one precious point.

The Floating Frog

I desperately searched my mental archives – so many contenders, so little dignity.

My first thought was the time when, at the age of four, my sister convinced me that the theme song from the old American TV series Casey Jones actually included my name in the lyrics.

I genuinely believed her that the chorus was singing:

♫ Steven and a Rowley ♫

rather than the far more logical line about a steam engine rolling along:

♫ Steamin' and a-rollin' ♫

I believed it so completely that I even managed to convince my friends. Soon enough, they were all belting out my personalised version with absolute confidence.

Then came the day my world collapsed.

There I was, perched proudly on our garden wall, playing the role of Casey Jones at the front of the imaginary Cannonball Express. All my mates sat behind me in perfect formation, chugging along on our concrete locomotive, singing my customised lyrics at full volume.

Cue: my older sister.

She possessed a natural – almost supernatural – talent for delivering maximum embarrassment with perfect timing.

Hearing our enthusiastic performance, she marched over like a disgruntled station master and brought the entire Cannonball Express to a screeching halt.

With great authority – and even greater satisfaction – she announced that the real lyrics did not include my name. Not even close.

I was devastated. Heartbroken.

Not only was my name not immortalised in the theme song of my favourite TV show, but every single passenger on that concrete locomotive immediately disembarked armed with fresh ammunition to mock me for the rest of my life.

News travelled faster than the Cannonball Express with a full head of steam. There was no escaping my embarrassment.

Back to the game.

Because there were no sisters or concrete locomotive passengers playing our game, nobody actually knew the answer.

So instead, I invited everyone to nominate what they believed were my most embarrassing moments – and then rate them on merit.

My wife Em didn't hesitate.

She shouted, with far too much enthusiasm: "The Flyscreen!"

Everyone else immediately agreed in perfect, damning unison.

The Flyscreen Incident

Elliot and his wife, Tyler, were unable to attend the final inspection of the house they were buying. In fact, because they were both working remotely, they ended up purchasing the place entirely on our recommendation – without ever setting foot inside.

So Em and I volunteered to do the final inspection before the keys were handed over.

We arrived at the house and were greeted by two real estate agents – car-salesmen types who had simply swapped hatchbacks for bricks and mortar.

After a quick handshake, we set off to inspect every crevice of the property in search of any imperfections that needed to be rectified, before exchanging contracts.

With the aid of modern technology, I FaceTimed Elliot so he could join us on a virtual tour of his soon-to-be home.

We wandered around the house, Elliot firing questions at every given opportunity:

Do the ceiling fans work?

Does the hot water system work?

Is the complementary lady cleaner charged and ready to go?

The complementary cleaner.

When I did the original open-house inspection with Elliot on FaceTime, I wandered past the outside laundry and, as I swung the camera around to show him inside, I spotted someone with their head buried deep in a cupboard, checking something.

Without thinking – because of course I didn't – I joked.

Me: "Look, the house even comes with a cleaner!"

And right on cue, the "cleaner" straightened up… revealing a smartly dressed woman of Asian descent who had absolutely heard me.

She wasn't a cleaner at all – she was another prospective buyer.

I have been ridiculed for that flippant comment ever since.

And rightly so. My timing is impeccable – just never in the way I want it to be.

Back to the inspection.

Elliot asked me to take him outside to check a few things at the front of the house.

So, I walked past Em and the two real estate agents, who were standing by the front door chatting. The main door was wide open, but the secondary flyscreen was closed. As I pushed the flyscreen outward to step outside, I casually commented to Elliot that it was a security screen – the mesh was metal, not fibre.

After a thorough virtual inspection, I headed back inside. I was talking to Elliot on my phone, looking at him instead of where I was going, when I discovered – far too late – that the flyscreen had a self-closing mechanism.

My world stopped instantly as I walked straight into the metal mesh.

Three things happened at once:

1. My knuckle, on the hand holding the phone, slammed into the screen with enough force to floor Mike Tyson.

2. Em and the real estate agents froze in perfect shock – silent, mouths open, wearing the exact expression of people who've just witnessed a ram-raid in slow motion.

3. I instinctively looked up, away from the phone, only to realise my forehead was pressed firmly against the mesh. In one smooth, cheese-grater-motion, I scraped a neat patch of skin from the centre of my forehead, triggering an immediate, dramatic trickle of blood down my face.

A deadly silence followed – broken only by a voice coming from my phone.

Elliot: "Dad? Did we just walk into a door?"

Another pause.

Me: "Yep."

Then total hysteria erupted from every direction.

I opened the flyscreen, revealing my newly decorated forehead to my audience. One of them – Em – lost all composure, collapsing into uncontrollable laughter, rendering her totally incapable of sympathy.

There I stood, a lone soldier in enemy territory, zero sympathy. The real estate agents remained frozen in time, their shocked expressions unchanged. Elliot was still on the other end of the phone, already relaying the disaster to his wife. And then there was Em – producing more tears of laughter than I was producing blood.

Me: "Yep, the security screen seems to work."

Real estate agent 1: "Good God! Are you okay?"

Me: "Yes! 'Tis but a scratch."

I was completely unaware of just how much blood was vacating my body via my forehead.

I brushed past my captive audience and headed for the bathroom at the far end of the house. Em followed behind me – unable to stand upright as she was doubled up with laughter. It was like Quasimodo trailing after Esmeralda. She had lost the ability to form actual words – reduced to sporadic bursts of squealing laughter.

Inside the bathroom, I looked in the mirror. There it was: a perfectly formed, one-inch round wound smack in the centre of my forehead. It looked as though I'd suddenly converted to a completely new religion.

Now, to stop the flow of blood.

Luckily, there was a roll of toilet paper on a cabinet. I quickly used a couple of sheets to press against the wound.

Nope. Not a chance.

I kept mopping, then flushing the blood-soaked sheets down the toilet.

Meanwhile, Em's attempts at sympathy kept getting interrupted by little spurts of concern, a squeal, and then full, helpless, wheezing laughter.

Five minutes on, and one whole roll of bog paper down, I finally stemmed the bleeding and restored what little dignity I had left.

I dabbed my brow with the sad, final scrap of paper as I shuffled out of the toilet, then, burning with embarrassment, trudged back toward the real estate agents. Em followed, still wheezing and utterly useless to society.

As I approached the real-estate agents, I could see genuine looks of concern.

Real-estate agent 1: "Oh my God! Are you OK? We were really concerned about you."

I opened my mouth to reply, but –

Real-estate agent 1: "Emma, we thought you were having an asthma attack."

For god's sake. Really?

Half my forehead was still embedded in the flyscreen mesh like a festive Christmas wreath, my dignity levels somewhere below zero, and their main concern was Em? Bastards.

Then their focus shifted to me – well, to my forehead, really. Their eyes widened, and the whole scene dissolved into something straight out of a comedy outtake: desperate attempts to stay professional, voices leaping octaves, eyes watering, and snorts escaping in short, guilty bursts as they tried to contain the laughter leaking out of them.

I thought, How rude. If they'd greeted Gandhi like this, it would've triggered worldwide religious demonstrations.

I turned to Em, hoping for some moral support.

She took one look at me and – in a pitch normally only detectable by dogs – squealed:

Em: "What the hell is that dangling from your forehead?

Please don't tell me that's toilet paper."

Yep. The final dab of my brow, unbeknownst to me, had decided to skin-graft itself to my forehead.

That was it. Like the final joke at a Billy Connolly performance, I left my audience unable to breathe, incapacitated by hysterical laughter.

Then I realised my audience also included Elliot – still on FaceTime – with the addition of his wife, Tyler. Snuggled up with a pack of popcorn, enjoying my impromptu slapstick comedy routine.

The Royal Nod of approval for the house inspection was my ticket to 'total-humiliation freedom'.

I hit the end-call button on my phone and dragged Quasimodo toward the car, with her complaining, "You nearly bloody killed me in there."

Ignoring the real-estate agents shouting "ENCORE!" behind us, we disappeared into the sunset – physically and mentally scarred for life.

Back to the game.

Having to relive the whole ordeal again, I agreed that yes, that was my most embarrassing moment. I was just about to hand my card over to Em as her reward for guessing correctly when –

Alfie began shaking his head, clearly disagreeing.

Alfie: "Nope. That's not your most embarrassing moment."

I looked at him, completely perplexed.

Alfie: "ANZAC Day?"

And just like that, my brain – and probably Elliot's – opened the never-to-be-opened drawer buried deep in the memory bank.

I handed my card to Alfie immediately for guessing correctly, praying – truly praying – that he wouldn't repeat the story at the table.

Nope. The story was told.

I closed my eyes, hoping my entire system would shut down until Alfie had finished retelling my most embarrassing moment of all time.

And so, in the grand tradition of the Loose Screw Society, I present to you…

The Remembrance Day- Best We Forget

Let's set the scene.

It's ANZAC Remembrance Day. I'm at the cemetery, waiting to acknowledge all the ex-servicemen who have passed away during the past year.

I'm emotional and proud all at once – especially because Elliot has the honour of playing the Last Post as the official bugler at the ceremony.

To ensure I have the perfect view of Elliot, I position myself right at the front, slightly to the left of the old soldiers waiting to pay their respects to fallen colleagues, medals proudly pinned to their jackets.

They're lined up in three rows, twenty in each row. Some standing, some sitting due to age and frailty. I look at each soldier paying their last respects to their comrades. I'm oozing admiration for these heroes, acknowledging the sacrifices they've made for their country. My eyes are already tearing up. It's a genuinely special moment.

People gather to my left as well, standing in quiet solidarity so these men will never be forgotten.

Then the Parade Commander, loud and clear: "COMPANY! ATTENTION!"

The old soldiers to my right immediately snap to attention, medals clanking as their feet hit the ground with surprising force.

Cue Private Dipstick.

At the exact same moment, I hear the same noise to my left.

That's odd, I think.

I slowly turn toward the source of the sound.

There – three more rows of old soldiers.

Behind me – two rows.

My worst fears kick in.

Shite. I'm standing in the middle of the official parade with absolutely nowhere to go.

I stare forward, completely out of my depth, with no idea how to escape this monumental disaster. Then I spot Elliot glaring at me from afar, mouthing, "What the fuck."

Now in full panic mode, I'm thinking, How the hell can I diplomatically remove myself from this catastrophic situation? What would Bear Grylls do?

The only escape route available is forward. My options:
1. Casually walk forward, stepping on the graves of fallen soldiers as I head for sanctuary.

Absolutely not.

> 2.   Shout, "Cover me, I'm going in!" then sprint until my legs give out.

Tempting, but no.

> 3.   Stand at ease and pray the Parade Commander doesn't order an about-turn and march.

Yes. This is the only survivable option.

At this point, I wanted the ground to open up and swallow me.

Although given the location, that was probably not the best wish to make.

I copied the stance of the soldier next to me. I slowly and discreetly move my heels together, hands by my side, standing upright as if I have a broom handle inserted up my bottom. I am now the proud owner of a military attention stance.

Wow, I think. I'm going to pull this off.

Parade Commander *(loud and clear)*: "STAND AT EASE!"

Bugger. This is not good news, as I have the rare gift of being half a beat out with the rest of the world.

As everyone moves their feet with military precision, I provide the echo a second later.

Then I realise my hands should now be behind my back. Again, in my world, I discreetly move them from my sides to behind me without anyone noticing.

Wrong. Elliot, eyes locked on me like a laser sight, shakes his head in disbelief.

The master of ceremonies begins the official service.

Meanwhile, I'm praying they won't make me salute – mainly because I only know the Benny Hill version. This is not a good time to be me.

Just when I think I'm safe –

Parade Commander *(loud and clear)*: "ATTENTION!"

Another mistimed echo rolls across the grounds, and my nightmare instantly goes up a notch. Everyone snaps into a salute.

And because if you think it, you do it... There I am, saluting too – paying respect to genuine heroes while stuck in full Benny Hill mode.

I'm sure that if Elliot could've swapped his bugle for the ceremonial rifle, he would've taken the shot.

So, there I stand – Private Dipstick – saluting as the names of fallen soldiers are read out, each one followed by the solemn strike of a bell.

Then comes The Ode.

Everyone joins in with:

"Lest We Forget."

The Parade Commander (booming across the silence): "BUGLER!"

Now it's Elliot's turn. His faultless playing of the Last Post is genuinely moving.

Then the minute's silence.

Thankfully, my internal screaming stays locked inside my body.

The silence breaks when Elliot begins the Reveille.

He finishes the final note, and an eerily peaceful stillness settles over the crowd.

Parade Commander *(loud and clear)*: "STAND AT EASE!"

A brief pause – then, with my perfectly timed echo:

"COMPANY DISMISSED."

Thankfully, I wasn't asked to march; that would definitely have created a scene from a Laurel and Hardy movie.

I truly believed I had pulled it off; I had successfully infiltrated a military parade with no formal training.

I had survived the most excruciating, embarrassing fifteen minutes of my life.

I headed straight for Elliot, hoping for a bit of emotional and moral support, only for him to greet me through gritted teeth with:

Elliot: "What the hell were you doing in the parade?"

Me _(joking)_: "They ambushed me!

Elliot shook his head in disbelief.

Me: "It could have been worse. I could have pretended to be their prisoner and put my hands on my head for the whole ceremony."

I tried to reassure Elliot.

Me: "Nobody noticed except you?"

Elliot _(through gritted teeth)_: "Got away with it? I don't think so!

Everyone else was in a suit or uniform proudly wearing their medals, and you! You were in jeans, trainers and a bloody hoodie! And, while everyone else was saluting correctly, you were? … I don't even know what you were doing".

Elliot exhausted of all possible compliments and superlatives-

Elliot: "You Absolute Twat".

At that exact moment, the Parade Commander started walking directly towards us.

I immediately knelt down and started to rearrange flowers on a nearby grave so he couldn't speak to me.

Once Elliot finished talking to him, I abandoned my emergency flower-arranging duties.

Me: "What did he say?"

Elliot: "He thanked me for being the bugler… and asked what regiment you had served in."

Me: "And what did you tell him?"

Elliot *(sarcastically)*: "I told him you were a fully-fledged member of the Welsh Artillery Northern Kombat Elite Regiment."

Me: "A WANKER?"

Elliot: "Absolutely."

Interlude:

I often wonder how modern-day society would react to an invasion.

The Dover Dingy Landings

Via the power of multimedia, I can already picture it: the moment the Russian army tries to invade Britain – secretly landing in inflatable warships on the beaches of Kent, under the bold cover of broad daylight on a hot summer's day.

Then, once the invasion is finally realised, the Ministry of Defence immediately steps aside and lets the British Demonstration Army take the lead.

No helmets.

No rifles.

Just hi-vis vests, reusable water bottles, and the unshakeable confidence of people who've spent years gluing themselves to historic works of art.

The front line forms instantly:

A thousand protestors marching toward Russian troops armed with nothing but banners, orange paint, high-resolution mobile phone cameras, and the kind of moral certainty that can stop traffic on the M25 for six hours.

Russian tanks roll in.

The demonstrators sit down.

Superglue comes out.

Within minutes, half the Russian armoured division is permanently bonded to a swarm of screaming first-year university students, all of whom genuinely believed they were turning up for an Answers to Life, the Universe and Everything practical exam.

The Russians, overwhelmed by British passive aggression, retreat immediately into their five-star hotels.

Sky News cuts live to the Ritz, where negotiations are underway.

The British delegation – waving Russian flags like overenthusiastic Eurovision fans – offers the bewildered Russian soldiers full British citizenship.

The Prime Minister stands proudly after declaring the nation "The United Kingdom of Russia," then turns to grin smugly at his immigration-policy critics.

The Russian leader, overwhelmed by this unexpected diplomatic triumph, rewards the British PM and his government with an all-inclusive holiday at one of Russia's notorious Arctic Circle holiday camps.

And so the Parliamentary delegation, having forgotten the actual lyrics, boards the plane humming the tune of Rule Britannia – confident, off-key, and entirely unaware of what they've just agreed to.

The End

Outerlude:

Where was I…

Has this episode stopped me from attending military commemorative services? Not on your life.

Lest We Forget

Truthing

If you've made it this far, congratulations – you're now an official member of the Loose Screw Society.

This grants you special privileges, chief among them: letting me speak freely to you.

Or, in this case… write freely.

According to the sacred scrolls of the Book-Writing Gods, this kind of book must contain no fewer than fifty thousand words.

Thankfully, they've allowed me to repeat a few – otherwise, you'd be holding a dictionary with all the meanings stripped out.

I briefly considered developing a writer's stutter to hit the word count.

But then I thought:

"Bugger it! Let's go-go-go for one more tale."

So, like a constipated person of written words – and questionable judgement – I'm about to try and squeeze out one final chapter.

Credit where it's due:

Special thanks to Nancy Sinatra,

Who – via her iconic anthem 'These Boots Are Made for Walkin'' – introduced me to the word Truthing.

I liked how it sounded, scribbled it down as a chapter title,

And – naturally – in classic Loose Screw style… decided to wing it.

So, to you, good people of the Society,

I present – hopefully – **'Truthing'**.

Mum's Motto

My mum always said, "Tell the truth". She lived it every day of her life.

I vowed to follow in her footsteps.

Unfortunately – one of us was not Truthing.

So, for your benefit, and to protect my mother's reputation – I'll now be rating my theatrical fibs on the *Truthing Scale:*

• *10 – The truth, the whole truth, and nothing but the truth.*

• *5 – Cheeky.*

• *0 – USA presidential-level lie. (Nixon – who did you think I meant?)*

What follows is a curated selection from a lifetime of questionable decisions, each rated for your convenience.

The Slide – Truthing or Not Truthing?

- *After my dive-from-the-top-of-the-slide incident, Ivor's mum let him keep the puppy – which he named Boner?*

Truthing Scale: 0

Come on, readers! There were no puppies. Ivor panicked when he saw me playing dodge-the-pedo and legged it, leaving me to fend for myself.

***

Believing – Truthing or Not Truthing?

- *Sharing a toilet cubicle with a senior girl mid-motion, gave me the ability to hold my breath so long... I could never drown?*

Truthing Scale: 5

- *God placing the uninvited nugget in my pants as a pre-emptive punishment for the Fantasia Angel incident?*

Truthing Scale: God Knows!

***

Christmas Party – Truthing or Not Truthing?

- *Twinkle – my glam-rock costume – was as real as you?*

Truthing Scale: 10

- *Pretending I didn't know who Wonder Woman was?*

Truthing Scale: 0

I spent hours trying to pause my VHS player at the exact frame where the radiant Lynda Carter was mid-spin, mid-outfit change, mid-magic.

Ah, the innocence of youth.

- *In an attempt to escape the humiliation of standing in front of a class wearing my football kit and 'foil-wrapped platform shoes'. Michelle the Fairy turned me into a frog in exchange for my marshmallow snowballs?*

Truthing Scale: 0

Under no circumstances would I ever share my marshmallow snowballs.

- *Having brokered a deal with Michelle in exchange for my Rola Cola instead, I spent the rest of the day sitting by the school fishpond with two Karens – Three Frogs in the Fountain?*

Truthing Scale: 5

Holton Road Primary School never had a fountain in its fishpond, or any other sort of water feature.

Come to think of it, the school didn't even have a fishpond.

***

Pea Shooterist – Truthing or Not Truthing?

Operation: Reconnecting the WANKERs

- *To avoid capture by Field Marshal Willie Schnapper, Pete and I took two and a half hours to reconnect with the WANKERs – despite HQ being only five minutes from the ambush site?*

Truthing Scale: 10

Terror makes you zigzag.

Bogeying – Truthing or Not Truthing?

> • *The triplets and a mother expressing milk like a water cannon?*

Truthing Scale: 5

There were no babies. Just a rusty pram frame with wheels, a pack of angry kids, and two lads with questionable judgement.

> • *Telling the owner of the Hillman Imp that we had no insurance?*

Truthing Scale: 5

We did. But we selfishly lied to protect our no-claims discount.

***

Conkering – Truthing or Not Truthing?

> • *Woolworths launched an actual advertising campaign featuring the versatile Windfield Tracksuit wearable shopping bags – "Fill Them, Wear Them" – hands-free shopping made possible?*

> *Disclaimer: Not suitable for cyclists*

Truthing Scale: 5

***

Nine Nails – Truthing or Not Truthing?

> The Freddy Krueger Incident

> • *The nurse seeing my novelty 3D pants and thinking I'd pooped myself?*

Truthing Scale: 5

Truth: I'd panicked, removed Sister Grapples pink knickers, and forgotten to put my own back on.

The desk nurse got an eyeful of my bare derrière.

Smoking – Truthing or Not Truthing?

- *Purple platform shoes, patch pocket trousers, long woollen cardigan, a bobbleless bobble cap, and enough Old Spice to fumigate a small village was definitely 70s cool?*

Truthing Scale: 10

Sunday-only bathing was a sacred tradition in the 70s.

We didn't smell bad.

We smelled… spicy.

***

Push Biking – Truthing or Not Truthing?

- *To Samuel L. Jackson, esteemed owner of the Ford Cortina:*
  I did 'not' embed my pedal into the driver's door?

Truthing Scale: 10

To the rest of the world:

Truthing Scale: 0

***

Motor Biking – Truthing or Not Truthing?

- *After Pete and I somehow turned our deafening Kawasaki stunt into an overnight stay at Linda's house – and failed to tell Mum the truth about our whereabouts –*
  I spent over an hour trying to convince her that my packet of Jelly Tots had remained sealed for the entire visit?

Truthing Scale: 10

- *From that day forward, I vowed, again, never to lie to her?*

Truthing Scale: 5

Driving – Truthing or Not Truthing?

- *The escapee driving my Cortina 1600E abandoned the car mid-police chase, vaulted a stone wall, tumbled five metres down a railway embankment, broke his ankle, and still managed to limp three miles along the tracks back to his house to avoid capture?*

Truthing Scale: 10

***

Nightclubbing at the Disco – Truthing or Not Truthing?

- *Extra strong mints may counteract the effects of alcohol – but they come with a flammable side effect?*

Truthing Scale: 5

***

Maturing at the Cherry Pop Golf Club – Truthing or Not Truthing?

- *I lost my virginity on a golf course?*

Truthing Scale: 0

Come on, people – it's a metaphor for life's journey.

A terrible one.

- *Beergoggle Flo moved into a house just around the corner from ours?*

Truthing Scale: 10

Karma clearly isn't done with me yet.

- *Florence is her real name?*

Truthing Scale: 0

Football Tackle – Truthing or Not Truthing?

- *Pete's left his wife and moved in with our goalkeeper?*

Truthing Scale: 0

Pete is still happily married to this very day.

- *Robbie - aka Rob the Knob - is a living legend, with comic timing worthy of his own Christmas Special?*

Truthing Scale: 10

***

Filthy Films – Truthing or Not Truthing?

- *Nan's starring role in this tale was one hundred percent accurate?*

Truthing Scale: 10 (Gold Level)

She could've easily shared the spotlight with Robbie in his Christmas Special - no script required.

***

A Proper Love Story – Truthing or Not Truthing?

- *The Gothic Chick is a carbon copy of Nessa from Gavin and Stacey. A bit slimmer, same hairdresser, same genuine Barry accent?*

Truthing Scale: 10

- *Em still wears her engagement ring – genuine tin. She refuses to take it off. It's a symbol of our everlasting love?*

Truthing Scale: 0

Within a month, it turned her finger green.

She tried everything to stop the reaction – but sadly for me (and splendidly for Em), I had no choice but to replace it.

Seven-carat diamond cluster ring later – we were engaged again.

Parenting – Truthing or Not Truthing?

- *The UK Government approached me about rolling out my Child of the Week scheme within their Early Years Development and Training programme?*

Truthing Scale: 5

- *I'm addicted to 'Twatism'?*

Truthing Scale: 10

***

Parading – Truthing or Not Truthing?

- *I have taken lessons on the art of ceremonial saluting – just in case?*

Truthing Scale: 0

I'm still a Benny Hill look-a-like, now with the urge to slap small bald men on the head.

***

Saved the Best for Last

The Conjoined Twins Existence – Truthing or Not Truthing?

- *Colin and Brian are conjoined brothers with their own agenda?*

Truthing Scale: 5 (very cheeky)

Alright, alright – they weren't literally conjoined.

They weren't even twins.

Just two brothers, born ten months apart, operating like a single unit. You never saw one without the other.

People always said they were joined at the hip. So technically… conjoined.

Truthing Scale: 10

The Floating Frog and All Its Tales – Truthing or Not Truthing?

All true, with a generous sprinkling of humour?

Truthing Scale: 10

Closing the Chapter

Mum always said, "Tell the truth."
And I've tried – honestly.

But if she were here reading this chapter, she'd look at me, shake her head, and say:

"Steven… Truthing Scale: 5."

And she'd be right.

She usually was.

Declaration of Chaos

So, dear members of the Loose Screw Society – keepers of chaos, connoisseurs of questionable taste, and proud defenders of the absurd – this is me, signing off.

I come armed with humour – not as a shield, but as a spotlight.

It masks the trauma, yes – but more importantly, it magnifies the embarrassment.

I know you've compared some of my tales. Rated them. Debated them. Possibly wept. Definitely winced.

That's your job.

Mine is to deliver them with reckless sincerity.

You've got your own stories to tell.

I just happen to tell mine louder – with more scares (physical and mental), and a lot more Epsom salts.

'Long live the Loose Screw Society - May our bolts never tighten'

YOU HAVE BEEN READING

The Floating Frog

Acknowledgement

To Em's dad – aka Michael Tunbridge, aka Mike, aka My Bestie. Grand Master of the Loose Screw Society.

Your total disregard for common sense is what inspired me to write these memoirs. Not so much an acknowledgement of thanks… more of a shared blame.

So, if anyone's looking for someone to hold accountable… I'm pointing at you.

Thank you, Bestie. x